The Sacred Scrolls

An Introduction to

Vedic Knowledge System

Compiled by,

PARAG M. BHALERAO

Understanding the basics about structure, content and topics discussed in the Vedic Knowledge System

THE SACRED SCROLLS

An Introduction to Vedic Knowledge System

Published on:

October 12, 2024

अश्विन शुल्क दशमी (दसरा) शके १९४६

Compiled by,

PARAG M. BHALERAO

Editing assistant,

GAURI BHALERAO

Published by:

Parag M Bhalerao

(USA)

DEDICATION

To those who tread the ancient paths, their hearts aflame with curiosity, this humble offering is dedicated.

In reverence to the Vedic Knowledge System, where syllables become cosmic bridges, we honor the luminous minds that shaped epochs. Let this dedication echo across time, resonating with the seers who whispered mantras to the winds.

To the Rishis, the celestial listeners, their eyes reflecting starlight, who drank from the cosmic chalice. Their visions, like constellations, guide us

To the Unbroken Lineage: From guru to disciple, across millennia, the Vedas flow—an eternal river. Let us honor the parampara—the sacred thread connecting us to the cosmic symphony.

To all of you, the Seekers of the knowledge that purifies and liberates— the self, the cosmos, and the spaces in between.

May this dedication be a beacon—a mantra whispered across lifetimes.

- Parag Bhalerao

A Note to Readers

Dear readers,

In the quietude of ancient forests, where the rustle of leaves echoes the whispers of sages, we embark on a journey—a pilgrimage across the sacred terrain of the Vedic knowledge system. Here, the cosmic and the mundane converge, and the syllables of eternity resonate.

The Vedas, those primordial hymns etched upon the fabric of existence, beckon us. Their roots plunge deep into the cosmic loam, nourished by the sap of timeless wisdom. As we step into this luminous expanse, let us unfurl the scrolls of antiquity, revealing the structure of knowledge that spans epochs and galaxies.

Beyond parchment and ink, the Vedas flow as an unbroken river. From Guru to Shishya, across millennia, they traverse oral realms. The Rishis, those seers who drank from the celestial chalice, entrusted their visions to the winds. And so, the Vedas remain—resonant, eternal.

As we embark, dear readers, let us honor the lineage "the Parampara" that carries these sacred verses. Let us listen to the rustle of ancient leaves, for they bear witness to the cosmic symphony.

May the Vedas guide us, like celestial compasses, toward the heart of existence. I am confident that you will find my interpretations insightful and valuable.

Parag Bhalerao

CONTENTS

Society that is aware of its rich knowledge heritage and cultural, can take pride in boldly represent itself in front of modern world.

It takes only a little bit of effort to know our glorious past.

BACKGROUND

"Access to the Vedas is the greatest privilege this century may claim over all the previous centuries" said American nuclear physicist J. Robert Oppenheimer, father of Atom Bomb. Many other renowned modern scientists and scholars have mentioned the Vedic literature to be of great value to the world.

Unlike common belief, Vedas are not merely Hindu religious books. Indian heritage of knowledge, which begins with Vedas and other texts, is an ocean of pure knowledge. This knowledge is relevant to everyone regardless of race or religion.

What Are Vedas

The word Veda (वेद) comes from the root word vid (विद्), which means "to know" and the word Veda indicates "knowledge". So essentially the ancient scripture called Vedas are nothing but books filled with a variety of knowledge. This knowledge was acquired by ancient Indian sages and

9

grouped in four books called Rigveda, Yajurveda, Saamveda and Atharvaveda.

Indian knowledge system classifies knowledge into two parts. Aparā vidyā (अपरा विद्या) and parā vidyā (परा विद्या). Aparā vidyā is considered common knowledge that is essential for day-to-day living. It is commonly available and easy to learn and acquire. Aparā vidyā is supreme knowledge about the creator or supreme consciousness. This is the knowledge about paramātmā or parabrahma or parameśvara or brahman, etc. Vedic knowledge is accepted to be the parā vidyā. The knowledge that is most powerful, always existed, never changing, and leads to liberation is available in Vedas.

Vedas are composed using Mantra (मन्त्र). These Mantras are believed to be revealed through breathing of the supreme consciousness.

Origin of Vedas

It is also important to note who the "authors" or "creators" of Vedas are. Vedas are said to be "Apaurusheya" (अपौरुषेय), which means not created or written by humans. Also, Vedas were not written by one sage or Rishi (ऋषी). Different Rishis at different times wrote different Mantras that formed Vedas. While these Rishis were extremely intelligent and accomplished, they were very humble. They proclaimed that the Mantras in Vedas were revealed to (or through) them by the supreme consciousness or Brahman. These Rishis "heard" the Mantras when they were in deep meditative state, also known as samādhi avasthā (समाधि

अवस्था). Rishis believed that they were merely an instrument used by the Brahman to reveal the Vedas. These Rishis did not take credit for composition of the Mantras. Since these Mantras were revealed to ancient sages, but not really composed by those sages those are called Apaurusheya.

Rishis through whom Mantras were revealed are known as Draṣṭā Rishis or seers for those Mantras. Again, it is important to understand that these were merely seers and not composers. As these Rishis "heard" these Mantras, they taught the Mantras to their disciples following the oral tradition. For this reason, Vedas are known as śruti (श्रुति), meaning "heard".

Later around 5000 BCE, Maharshi Vyas (महर्षी व्यास) compiled all the Mantras, organized and documented those in four Vedas. To honor his work, Maharshi Vyas is called Veda Vyas.

After organizing the text in four Vedas, Maharshi Vyas taught each of the Vedas to one of his disciples. Rigveda was taught to Paila, Yajurveda to Vaishampayana, Saamveda to Jaimini, and Atharvaveda to Sumantoo. These great disciples preserved Vedic knowledge and heritage through oral tradition. They studied and preserved not only the text, but also the intricacies of chanting, pronunciations, intonations, etc.

These Vedas are ancient, and their dates are not easily established. Many scholars have estimated different periods for the origin of Vedas. Based on astronomical references, Dr. P. V. Vartak calculated scientific dating of Vedas. This dating goes way back to 24,000 BCE.

Importance of Vedas

Indian belief system accept Vedas are root of Dharma[1]. vedo dharmasya mūlam (वेदो धर्मस्य मूलम्) says Manu Smriti[2]. Various duties, dos and don'ts, prescriptions described in Veda are nothing but Dharma. Vedas are to be studied with kartavya buddhi (कर्तव्य बुद्धि) or with sense of duty and with no attachments. They inspire everyone to do the work or take actions. In Vedic context work is nothing but Yajna. However, Yajna should not be confused with current age Yajna where fire is lit in enclosed area formed with bricks and offerings are made in the fire. While that is one form of Yajna, that is not the only form. Any good and dharmic action performed with sincerity, focus and purpose can qualify as Yajna. Rigveda is the root text for Yajna based society (or Sanatan Dharma).

Vedic knowledge and study system believes the principle called "Yet Pinde, Tat Brahmande" (यत् पिण्डे तद् ब्रह्माण्डे), which means "All that is within you (your body), is also in the universe around you". Our body is a miniature representation of the universe. Pinda indicates microcosm and Brahmanda indicates macrocosm. Just like a small portion or even an atom of an element is sufficient to study properties and characteristics, the microcosm is sufficient to know all about the macrocosm. For this

---

[1] Word Dharma is loosely translated as Religion by western languages, which is not be best translation. There is no equivalent word for Dharma in many non-Indian languages.

[2] The Manusmriti (मनुस्मृति) is a book of ideas on how society should run. This will be discussed later in smriti discussions.

reason, Vedic scholars focus on meditation and self-discovery to know more (or all) about the universe and external objects. This also is the reason, why carious natural entities in the universe are equated to various body organs, the sun to eyes as an example.

Yajna is also a process of establishing a connection between the Pinda and the Brahmanda. In other words, the process of learning about the supreme reality or supreme consciousness is called Yajna.

Dharma

One that inspires people towards good deeds (सत्कर्म) is nothing but Dharma. This is the inspiration one can get from Veda and hence Vedas are also foundation for Dharma.

There are many other texts that provide guiding principles in Hindu (or Sanatan) belief system. All other texts are based on knowledge available in Vedas. Authorities such as Manu, Jaimini, Jabal, etc. have clearly stated that if there is a conflict between sayings in various other books and Vedas, then Vedas should be treated as standards.

Jaimini Rishi clearly states "śruti-smṛtivirodhe tu śrutireva garīyasī (श्रुति-स्मृतिविरोधे तु श्रुतिरेव गरीयसी)" meaning, if there is a conflict between Vedic (śruti) and other (smṛti) statements, Vedas should be considered as standard.

Maharshi *yājñyavalkya* also clarifies in his own smṛti that any actions and duties described in smṛti are allowed to be followed only if those are not against Veda.

If we leave aside Vedas, there is no other authoritative text in Hindu Dharma that provides clarification and information about its culture, policies, etc.

Chandas

We can find both proses and poetic verses in Vedas. In both cases, the compositions are bound in specific Chanda (छन्द) or rhyme. Chandas are categorized by number of syllables, types of vowels, etc. Each Mantra has a Chanda based on how that Mantra was revealed (or heard by Sages). In Vedic text, there are seven Chandas viz.,

- gāyatrī (गायत्री)   6 + 6 + 6 + 6   = 24 syllables
- uṣṇik (उष्णिक्)   8 + 8 + 12   = 28 syllables
- anuṣṭup (अनुष्टुप्)   8 + 8 + 8 + 8   = 32 syllables
- bṛhatī (बृहती)   8 + 8 + 12 + 8   = 36 syllables
- paṃkti (पंक्ति) 8 + 8 + 8 + 8 + 8   = 40 syllables
- triṣṭup (त्रिष्टुप्) 11 + 11 + 11 + 11   = 44 syllables
- jagatī (जगती)   12 + 12 + 12 + 12   = 48 syllables

Mantras

Various verses in Vedas are known as Mantras. Mantras are different than verses or śloka (श्लोक). One of the key aspects of chanting the Mantras is that the Mantras are supposed to be chanted exactly the way those were heard by the Rishis. The intonation of various syllables is of great importance while chanting the Mantras. Teaching or chanting

Mantras without proper intonation is considered sinful.

Today we hear many artists and singers singing Mantra in various tunes. This is not allowed by the rules of Veda.

Many places within Vedic literature it is mentioned that chanting Mantras by knowing and following Rishis, Chanda, Devata and Swara (tone) can bring great benefits, while not doing so can cause more harm.

Ancient practice follows reciting Mantras with proper intonation (tone, pitch or accent). In ancient practice, there were eighteen distinct tones being followed. Over period of time, these eighteen tones have been forgotten. Today there is no known person who can chant Mantras using all eighteen tones. Current scholars follow three tones while chanting Mantras. In written script the tones or pitch is indicated by horizontal line under for lower pitch, vertical line above for higher pitch and no line for normal pitch.

- The higher pitch is called udātta (उदात्त), which is basic and unchangeable accent
- The low pitch is called anudātta (अनुदात्त)
- The normal pitch is called Svarita (स्वरित)

While learning a proper way of chanting Mantras, many teachers ask students to follow up, down or sideways movement of hands.

Scholars are worried that improper pronunciation is making Mantras 'spoiled' and not as fruitful.

Knowledgeable Person

While many people claim to be authorities or knowers of Veda, there is a clear description of who can be called Knowledgeable about Veda. People who are aiming to gain knowledge of Vedas must study Veda in its entirety including Brahmanas and Upanishads, and with proper understanding of meaning of these texts. Such person should be initiated through Upanayana ritual, study Veda(s) from qualified Guru and get "certified" by the Guru. Then such person is called śrotriya (श्रोत्रिय). Without becoming a śrotriya, a person is not qualified to call self as knowledgeable. Just old age, possession of wealth, influence in society, etc. are not qualifications to be knowledgeable in Veda(s).

Vedic Devata (Deities)

At a cursory look it appears that various Mantras in Vedas are in praises of various powers or energies. These powers are Devatas for respective Mantras. Examples of these Devatas include Agni (fire), Vayu (wind), Surya (sun), etc. This leads many people to think that Vedic texts discuss polytheism. However, it is important to understand that all such Devatas are forms of supreme consciousness or Brahman.

The universe is composed of five basic elements viz. Space, Air, Fire, Water, and Earth. These five elements, different forms of the elements and energies associated with these elements are addressed as Devatas in Vedic text.

Further, Vedic Devatas are of various classes. These include natural forces, emotional forces, and others. Natural (or physical) forces include

Varuna, Surya, Vishnu, Parjanya, Usha, Agni, Soma, Vayu etc. Emotional forces or energies include Kaamdevata, Mana, Shraddha, etc. While the other Devatas include Yaksha, Gandharva, Apsara, etc.

This type of polytheism helps people to believe that everything in the nature, everything around them and everything within them is some form of Devata. This helps society live harmoniously with nature and each other.

Chanting Mantras invokes specific Devatas. This does not mean that Devatas appear in human form from the Yajna by chanting Mantras. It simply means that chanting Mantras provides energy (vibrations) for various elements to manifest in different forms. For example, when we hear that the Prajanya (rain) Devata appears from Yajna, it means that by following certain process, it is possible to get rain.

Vedic Knowledge

As we discussed, the word Veda means Knowledge. Various kinds of knowledge are discussed in Vedas. Modern science tries to capture evidence to the best possible extent to prove any theory, however many theories are still based on some key assumptions that can't be proven. The Vedic literature focuses more on realization of the knowledge rather than focusing on assumptions and evidence.

Reading about some of the inventions discussed in Vedic texts is absolutely fascinating and beyond the reach of modern science today.

STRUCTURE OF INDIAN KNOWLEDGE SYSTEM

Even tough Vedas are at the core of Indian knowledge system, there are many other texts that are associated with and evolved from Vedas. We will discuss and understand basic aspects of these texts.

Just like many branches spring out of a tree, many branches of knowledge sprung out of Vedas. The following tree illustrates the structure of knowledge system.

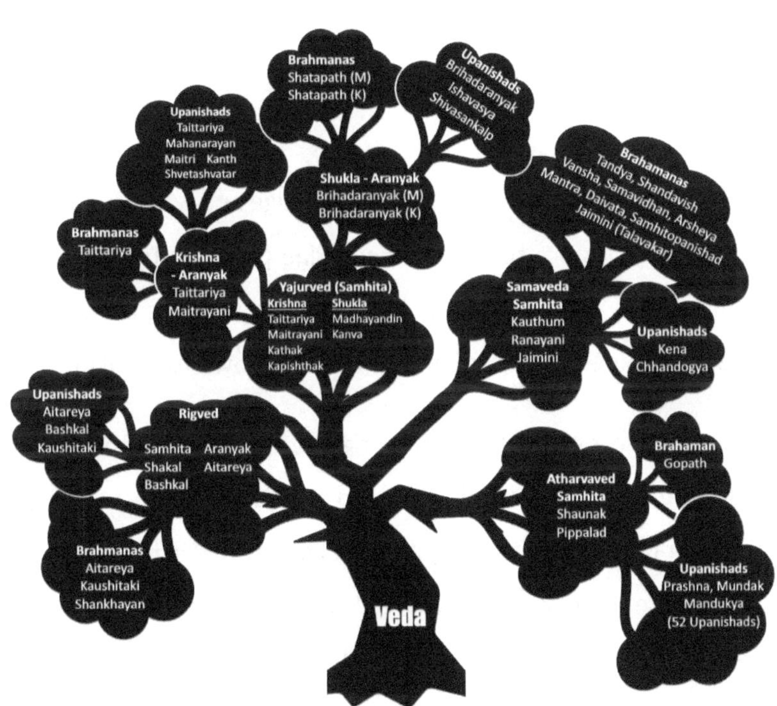

Shruti and Smriti

As we discussed earlier, Vedas were revealed to various Rishis. Since those Rishis 'heard' Vedas and continued to spread the knowledge through an oral tradition, Vedas are called as Shruti (or heard) books.

Based on this revealed knowledge in Vedas, many Rishis provided additional clarifications, commentaries or built additional supporting or simplified documents. Rishis remembered Vedic knowledge and built additional texts on that foundation. Such additional texts fall under Smriti (or remembered) category.

Vedas

The Vedas are ancient Indian texts of knowledge and wisdom. Sanatan or Hindu philosophies are based on knowledge provided by Vedas. Vedas are composed in Vedic Sanskrit, which is different than current Sanskrit. Vedas are the oldest literature and scriptures known to mankind.

Vedic knowledge is eternal. It has no origin or no end. It is knowledge that always existed and will continue to exist. It is believed that originally there was only one Veda and eventually it was divided in four parts. These four parts are four Vedas know today. These are the Rigveda, the Yajurveda, the Samaveda and the Atharvaveda. Around 5000 BCE, Maharshi Veda Vyasa organized Mantras in these four Vedas. Later he taught these four Vedas to his four disciples to further spread the Vedic knowledge. He taught the Rigveda to Pail, the Yajurveda to Vaishampayan, the Samaveda to Jaimini and the Atharvaveda to Darun.

Many ancient references mention only three Vedas viz. the Rigveda, the Yajurveda and the Samaveda. These three Vedas together are called Vedatrayi. The Atharvaveda is not mentioned in Vedatrayi. Naturally a question arises about what is this fourth Veda, the Atharvaveda? Atharvaveda is not a root construct like other three Vedas. Atharvaveda was composed by Rishi Atharva. He studied three Vedas and combined various Mantras from these three Vedas for the purpose of specific.

Further, each Veda has four sections called the Samhitas, the Aranyakas, the Brahmanas, and the Upanishads.

Samhitas

Word Samhita means collection. As Maharshi Veda Vyas organized the Vedic knowledge in four Vedas, he collected few Mantras specific to a specific activity together. This collection became Samhita for respective Veda. Mantras in Samhitas are used while performing yajñas. In any yajña, there are four main parts.

- Inviting Gods
- Making offerings in the yajña
- Songs for praising Gods
- Observing overall process of the yajña

Rishis involved in performing the yajña are called ṛtvik (ritvik or ऋत्विक) and they are of four types, each corresponding to one activity and one of the Vedas. Mantras chanted by ṛtviks correspond to Samhitas from respective Vedas. These ṛtviks have different names based on activities they perform in a yajña.

ṛtviks	Responsibilities	Veda / Samhita
Hotā (होता)	Chant Mantras to invite the yajña devatas	ṛgveda saṃhitā (ऋग्वेद संहिता)
Adhvaryu (अध्वर्यु)	Make offerings in the yajña	yajurveda saṃhitā (यजुर्वेद संहिता)
udgātā (उद्गाता)	Sing praises to the yajña Gods to please them	sāmaveda saṃhitā (सामवेद संहिता)
brahmā (ब्रह्मा)	Carefully observe (supervise) entire process of the yajña by leveraging knowledge of all Vedas	atharva saṃhitā (अथर्व संहिता)

Brahmanas

While Samhitas consist of core Mantras, those are followed by Brahmanas. Brahmanas provide additional explanation about Mantras and describe Yajna activities and process in more details. Religious as well as philosophical aspects of Mantras are discussed in Brahmanas. Primary focus of Brahmanas is related to Yajna rituals and secondary focus is on knowledge of the Brahman. Scholars consider Brahmanas to be limbs of Vedas. Sayanacharya says, whatever is not Mantra portion in Vedas, is Brahmanas and whatever is not Brahmana portion of Vedas, is Mantras.

Brahmanas provide additional explanation of Mantras. Without Brahmanas, understanding Mantras would be difficult. Many Mantras briefly mention some given concept, but Brahmanas provide more explanation about such concepts. Details about social structure, Devata, etymological interpretations of words in Mantras, etc. are also found in Brahamanas.

Primary Brahmanas associated with respective Vedas are as follows,

Veda	Brahman	
Rigveda	• Aitareya	• Kaushitaki
	• Shankhayan	
Yajurved (White)	• Shatapath (M)	• Shatapath (K)
Yajurved (Black)	• Taittariya	
Saamaved	• Tandya	• Mantra
	• Shandavish	• Daivata
	• Vansha	• Samhitopanishad
	• Samavidhan	• Jaimini (Talavakar)
	• Arsheya	
Atharvaved	• Gopath	

Aranyakas

Aranya means jungle. Aranyaka indicates group of Mantras that are chanted in the jungle or away from populated residential areas. These Mantras were chanted by Rishis to understand secret and sacred knowledge related to Yajnas. Aranyakas are considered appendices of Brahmana texts.

Aranyakas describe rituals from various perspectives including philosophical speculations. Many believe that Aranyakas focus on karma-kanda (कर्मकाण्ड) or ritualistic action/sacrifice. At the same time few others

believe that Samhitas and Brahmanas focus on karma-kanda, and Aranyakas and Upanishads focus on jnana-kanda.

These being ancient texts, there are various opinions from various scholars and there is no clear description to distinguish between Aranyakas and Brahmanas.

Upanishads

The Upanishads (उपनिषद् Upaniṣad) are later parts of Vedic texts. The word Upanishad means sit (stay) near the Guru and learn. Upa indicates 'near', Ni indicates 'with definite purpose' and Sad/Sat indicates 'sit'. Upanishad texts are in the form of dialogue between a teacher and disciple(s), where disciple(s) sit near the Guru with the intention of learning and acquire the knowledge from the teacher. Upanishads for last parts of Vedic literature hence also known as Vedānta. Upanishads are mostly the concluding parts of the Brahmanas and Aranyakas of respective Veda. Upanishads discuss wide range of topics including self-knowledge, meditation, philosophy and so on, however their focus is mostly on self-knowledge. Upanishads discuss the relationship between Atman and Brahman in great details.

Every Veda has its own set of Upanishads. While there are many Upanishads, there are 108 Upanishads that are commonly accepted and known today. Out of these, there are few that are considered as "Pradhan Upanishads" or main or principal Upanishads. Different groups differ on which Upanishads fall under principal category. Adi Shankaracharya has written commentaries on these main Upanishads.

The ten Principal Upanishads include:

Ved	Principal Upanishads	Other Upanishads
Rigveda	• Aitareya	• Bashkal
		• Kaushitaki
Yajurveda (Black)	• Taittariya	• Mahanarayan
	• Katha	• Maitri Kanth
		• Shvetashvatar
Yajurveda (White)	• Brihadaranyak	• Shivasankalp
	• Ishavasya (Isha)	
Saamveda	• Kena	
	• Chhandogya	
Atharvaveda	• Prashna	• (52 Upanishads)
	• Mundak	
	• Mandukya	

Different Upanishads are composed in different combinations of prose and verse formats. Additional details about Upanishads are discussed under sections related to respective Vedas.

Spread of Vedic Literature

There are several texts associated with Vedic literature. The table below provides a quick snapshot of the spread of the Vedic literature,

	Rigveda	Yajurveds (W)	Yajurveda (B)	Samaveda	Atharvaveda
Original Branches	21	15	86	1000	99
Available Branches	Shakala Bashkala	Kanva Madhyandina	Taittariya Maitrayani Kathak Kapishthal	Kauthum Ranayaneeya Jaiminiya	Pippalada Shaunak
Brahmanas	Aitareya Kaushitaki	Shatapatha	Taittariya	Panchavinsha Shadvinsha Saamavidhana Aarsheya Daivata, Vansha, Chandogya	Gopath
Aranyakas	Aitareya Shankhyana	Brihadaranyaka	Taittariya	Talavakar	
Upanishada	Aitareya Kaushitaki Bashkala	Ishavasya	Taittariya Maitrayani Kathak Mahanarayan Shvetashvatar	Chandogya Kena	Prashna Mandukya Mundaka
Shraut Sutras	Ashvalayan Shankhyan	Katyayan	Apastanb Boudhayan Hiranyakeshi Vaghula Bharadvaj Vaikhanasa	Khadir Latyayan Drahyayan	Vaitan
Grihya Sutras	Ashvalayan Shankhyan	Paraskar	Apastanb Boudhayan Hiranyakeshi Katha Vaikhanasa	Khadir Gaubhil Gautam	Kaushik
Dharma Sutras	Vaishshtha		Apastanb Boudhayan Hiranyakeshi	Gautam	
Upavedas	Ayurveda	Dhanurveda		Gandharvaveda	Sthapatya Itihaas,* Puran*

* some texts refer to Itihaasas and Puranas as Upavedas

Upavedas

While Vedas have comprehensive knowledge about many topics, there are additional or supplementary scriptures called the Upavedas. Upavedas extract applied knowledge related to specific area of expertise. Commonly accepted Upavedas are,

- Ayurveda comes from Rigveda (Atharvaveda per Sushrut)
- Dhanurveda comes from Yajurveda.
- Gandharvaved comes from Samaveda.
- Shilpaveda comes from Atharvaveda.

Focus Areas of Upavedas

The table below provides brief information about the focus areas of these four Upavedas.

Upaveda	Focus Area
Ayurveda	Ayurveda covers science related to health and medicine. Ayuh means age or life and Veda means science. Focusing on healthy way of life and suggesting natural remedies for diseases, Ayurveda has established its importance even in modern society.
Dhanurveda	Dhanurveda focuses on military affairs and warfare. Knowledge about various weapons and how to use those weapons is discussed in Dhanurveda.

Gandharvaveda	Gandharvaveda focuses on topics related to music. It describes Raga, Sura, Taal, etc. Gandharvaveda also covers skills of acting and stage performance, called as Natya Shastra.
Shilpaveda	Shilpaveda, also known as Sthapatyaveda, deals construction related aspects including planning, designing, and construction of houses, villages, and cities. Vaastu Shastra, followed in modern society has its origin in Shilpaveda.

Vedangas

Vedanga or "the limbs of the Vedas" provide six disciplines associated with Vedic knowledge.

It is not clear when these six Vedangas were formed. However, as scholars started finding it difficult to understand archaic and difficult Vedic text, around middle of the first millennium BCE, the Vedangas were formed. For a scholar to learn and understand any Veda, learning all six vedangas along with one or more Vedas is important. One who has mastered four Vedas and six Vedangas is known as Dashagranthi Brahmin.

Six Vedangas and topics discussed in those include,

Vedanga	Topics
Shiksha	Shiksha text deals with phonetics and pronunciation. This focuses Sanskrit alphabets and the way words are combined and expressed in a Vedic recitation.
Chhandas	Chhandas describe poetic meter. This includes analyzing the number of syllables per verse, and any patterns within those verses.
Vyarkarana	Vyarkarana provides knowledge as well as rules related to grammar and linguistics.
Nirukta	Nirukta includes study of etymology and explanations of meanings of words that are archaic.
Kalpa	Kalpa privides details about instructions related to ritual. Various rituals related to weddings, births deaths and other life events, are discussed in Kalpa.
Jyotisha	Jyotisha covers study of astronomy and astrology to decide auspicious times to guide rituals and timekeeping.

Itihaas

In common translation Itihaas means History. However, Itihaas has much more significant meaning. Many of historic events and stories are considered as myths by modern society. Itihaas means "so indeed it was" or "so indeed it happened". Itihaas gives detailed description of various events happened in the past. Various astronomical, social, geological and other references are included in Itihaas texts.

Even though many historic events have taken place, from Vedic literature perspective, two books are accepted as Itihaas books, viz. Ramayana and Mahabharat. Due to the vast amount of knowledge available in these two books, many consider these two books as Pancham Veda or the fifth Veda. Scholars admit that it is difficult to understand core philosophy in Vedic text, without studying Itihaas books.

Ramayana:

Ramayana describes life, events, and related stories of Lord Rama. There are several versions of Ramayana available today, however the Valmiki Ramayana composed by Maharshi Valmiki is the most ancient one and is regarded as Itihaas. Most other Ramayanas are devotional books composed by various sages and devotees.

In addition to being an Itihaas book, Valmiki Ramayana is also the first biggest poetic text that was written.

Story of Ramayana:

The kingdom of Ayodhya was ruled by a very pious king Dasharatha, who had three wives and four sons, Rama, Lakshmana, Bharata and Shatrughana. Rama, son of Kausalya was not just eldest but also an ideal and perfect son. Rama completed his education in Ashrama of Sage Vasistha. After completing his education, Rama (along with his brothers) came back to Ayodhya. Sage Vishvamitra asked King Dasharatha to send

Rama with him to protect his Yajna rituals in the forest. During that period, Sage Vishvamitra tough various additional skills and sacred knowledge to Rama.

When he comes of age, Rama married Sita, the princess of King Janaka. King Dasharatha was about to crown Rama as the crown prince. However, Bharata's mother Kaikeyi, who resented Rama for being the crown prince. She calls up three free wishes that that Dasharatha had granted her and asks for Rama to be exiled for fourteen years and her son Bharata be made crown prince instead. The devastated Dasharatha had no choice and Rama left for exile, accompanied by Sita and Lakshmana. During his journey and stay in the forest, the two brothers helped many people and hermitages while destroying many demons.

Surphanaka, a female rakshasi (demoness) became enamored of Rama and is wounded by Lakshmana while trying to kill Sita. She ran to her brother Khara and asked him to avenge her. However, Khara and his army got defeated by Rama and Lakshmana. The only survivor ran to the kingdom of Lanka and begged Surphanaka's brother, Ravana to avenge them. Ravana had heard of Sita's beauty, and he decided to abduct her. Using trickery and magic, he managed to lure Rama and Lakshmana away from Sita and kidnaped her, taking her away to Lanka. A warrior from bird tribe, Jatayu stopped Ravana and fought with him, the Ravana slayed Jatayu.

Rama and Lakshmana traveled far and wide searching for Sita. Eventually, they met band of vanaras who pledged to help them. Hamunana, one of the mighty varana warriors, became Rama's staunch devotee. The vanaras seek out traces of Sita and found her in Lanka. Hanuman flew to Lanka and confirmed that Sita the same. He contacted Sita and informed her of Rama's whereabouts, promising that they will be back to rescue her.

Rama, Lakshmana and the vanar army built a bridge from India to Lanka. They traveled to Lanka, where an epic battle followed between the armies. Ravana was finally killed by Rama, and Sita was freed. They returned to Ayodhya, where Bharata returned the crown to Rama.

Lessons from Ramayana:

Apart from being a great depiction of historic events, Ramayana story teaches us many important life lessons. Importance of Dharma, duties, righteousness, emotions, relationships, and many other aspects can be learnt from this great epic. Some of the important lessons from Ramayana include,

- Truth and dharma always wins
- Unity is strength
- Commitment to our duties and responsibilities will bring glory
- Always stay on the path of righteousness
- Always remain humble
- Treat everyone with love and respect
- Build good acquaintances and alliances
- Learn to forgive

Mahabharata

Mahabharata, the second Itihaas book, describes a fight between good and bad tendencies through story of two families in Kuru dynasty, the Kauravas and the Pandavas. Maharshi Veda Vyasa, who was contemporary to Mahabharata era, has written the epic Mahabharata which was earlier called as Jaya.

One of the Holy books of Hinduism, The Bhagvad Geeta, is part of the epic Mahabharata. A dialog between Lord Krishna and his disciple, Arjuna, enlightens the readers about how to righteously deal with various life situations.

Story of Mahabharata

Mahabharata narrates a story of two sets of paternal first cousins, the Pandavas, five sons of the deceased king Pāṇḍu and the Kauravas, one hundred sons of blind King Dhṛtarāṣṭra. They became bitter rivals and opposed each other in war for possession of Bharata. Throughout the story, many characters pursue number of individual agendas in addition to numerous personal conflicts, ethical puzzles, subplots, and plot twists.

One of the important most figures throughout the Mahabharata is Lord Krishna who was also a cousin of Pandavas. Lord Krishna is avtara of Lord Vishnu who descended to earth in human form to rescue Law, Good Deeds, Right, Virtue and Justice and to establish the Dharma. During the Mahabharata war, he became Arjuna's mentor and charioteer.

Dhritarashtra, the blind king, was not only blind physically, but also his love for his wicked son, Duryodhana. Yudhishthira, the eldest of the

Pandavas played a game of dice with Kauravas and lost his entire kingdom, his brothers, himself as well as his wife Draupadi. After that, Kauravas humiliated all the Pandavas and physically abused Draupadi. Kauravas drove the Pandavas into twelve years of wilderness followed by one year in disguise, without getting identified. After that they could have their kingdom back.

The Pandavas fulfilled their part of that bargain, but Duryodhana refused to give the kingdom back to Pandavas. After several attempts of peaceful discussions, the war became necessary for Pandavas to win their kingdom back.

The Bhagvad Geeta, the most famous sermon of all time, Krishna's teachings to Arjuna accompanied by a demonstration of his divinity to his Arjuna occurred just before the war began.

The Pandavas won the eighteen-day battle. The victory was won by the Pandavas slaying four most respected men namely Bhishma, Dronacharya, Karna and Shalya.

Lessons from Mahabharata:

Entire story of Mahabharata demonstrated various qualities and good as well as bad tendencies of humans. The impact of these tendencies is a great learning for every human being even today. Some of the important lessons from Mahabharata include,

- Attachments make us blind
- Ego leads to destruction
- We can't run away from our duties

- Have faith in God and good
- Mind is most powerful weapon

Puranas

The word Purana means something that is ancient. Over the generations, Puranas have helped spread the Vedic knowledge to common people using simple story format.

Brahma acquired the supreme knowledge and passed it on to his four sons named named Sanaka, Sanandana, Sanatana, and Sanatkumara. Puranic texts describe that these four sons roam the universe as children. Sage Narada acquired this knowledge from Sanatkumara and Sage Narada passed that knowledge to Ved Vyasa. Ved Vyasa organized that knowledge in eighteen books which are called Puranas and Upa-Puranas.

Puranas describe ancient stories that encourage humans to stay on the path of devotion. Puranas are defined as,

सर्गश्च प्रतिसर्गश्च वंशो मन्वन्तराणि च | वन्शानुचरितञ्चैव पुराणं पञ्च लक्षणम् ||

sargaśca pratisargaśca vaṃśo manvantarāṇi ca |
vanśānucaritañcaiva purāṇam pañca lakṣaṇam ||

Descriptions of Sarga (creation of the universe), Prarisarga (delusion of the universe), Vansh (dynasty of the universe), Manvantara (description of Manus and Manvantaras) and Vanshanucharita (description of major kings and their dynasties), are five attributes of Puranas. However, in Puranas we find descriptions of various other topics as well.

Importance of Puranas

Puranas provide Vedic knowledge in simple words for easier understanding of common people. Most of the teachings are in story forms and include detailed descriptions of various ancient events. Knowledge spread by Puranas typically follows devotional path.

INTRODUCTION TO RIGVEDA

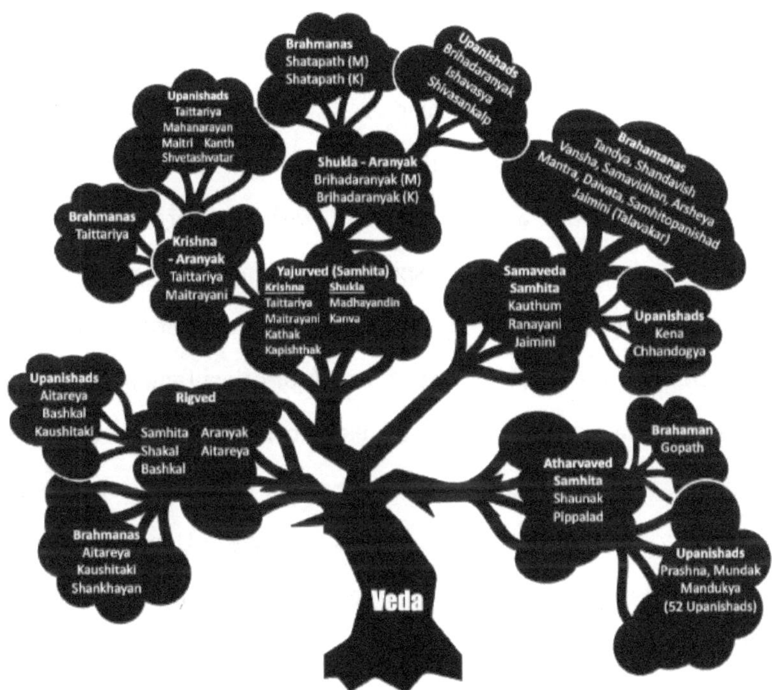

Background

The Rigveda is one of the four Vedas and accepted to be the first Veda. On grounds of both language and content, the Rigveda is the oldest of the four and foundational for the others. The second oldest is the Atharvaveda, a text that in some ways continues the compositional style of the Rigveda (and contains many repetitions from the Rigveda), but whose contents consist in large part, of personal spells and healing charms. Despite its age and affinity with Rigvedic poetic practice, it stands somewhat apart from the religious system of the Vedic period. In contrast, the other two Vedas, the Yajurveda and the Sāmaveda, form a ritually associated trio with the Rigveda, with each providing the ritual script for a different part of the spoken liturgy and for a different priest active in the joint ritual system of the middle Vedic period. The Rigveda was the source for the recitations of the Hotar priest (and assistants); the Yajurveda contained the formulas linked to ritual actions, which were principally carried out by the Adhvaryu priest (and assistants); and the Sāmaveda comprised the chants performed by the Udgātar priest (and assistants). We will have occasion to refer to all three other Vedas particularly in chapter 10.

The Rigveda consists of 1028 hymns, called sūktas meaning "well- well said". While common belief is that the sūktas are praises to Gods, these are not merely praises. There is a deep scientific meaning to many of these sūktas. It requires a careful study of various words, the meanings of those words, and the context or subject of the sūkta to reveal the real meaning. The sūktas consist of few verses or richas. Different sūktas have different number of richas and each richa is composed in specific meter or chhanda.

Verses in Rigveda are called richas, which comes from the word ṛc (rik) (ऋग् or ऋक्), hence the Veda is called Rigveda.

Different richas are revealed by different sages or seers. In many cases the entire sūkta is revealed by single seer, but that is not always the case. While many seers have not even mentioned their names, there are over 200 seers named in various sūktas.

Poorva Mimamsa Darshan text by Maharshi Jaimini provides a clear definition of ṛc (rik) as a composition that has deep and significant meaning that is bound in specific Chhanda. While chanting any mantra (or sūkta), it is important to know and recite name of the seer, the chhanda, the deity, etc.

In Vedic era, there were several branches of Rigveda, but most of those are lost over a period. The Rigveda Samhitas that are available today are Shakal Samhita (from lineage of Sage Shaunaka) and Kaushitaki Samhita.

Rigveda Samhita

Patanjali mentions 21 branches (shakha) of Rigveda Samhita, however today only Shakal Samhita is available. Shakal Smahita comes from Shakalya, who was 8th generation disciple of Veda Vyasa.

Rigveda construct is available in two formats, the Octet construct (अष्टक रचना) and the Mandala construct (मण्डल रचना).

The Octet construct is assumed to be more ancient and is easier to chant or recite. However, it does not present the best way to understand meaning of the Richas. The entire Samhita of Rigveda consists of eight Octets. Each Octet consists of eight chapters (अध्याय). Five Richas make one group called Varga (वर्ग) and each chapter has many such groups. By teaching one Varga every day, entire study of the Rigveda is completed in eight years. Details of the Octet construct are as follows,

Octet	Chapters	Vargas (Groups)	No. of Sūktas	No. of Richas (Mantras)
1	8	265	121	1370
2	8	221	119	1147
3	8	225	122	1209
4	8	250	140	1289
5	8	238	129	1263
6	8	331	135	1730
7	8	248	116	1263
8	8	246	146	1281
Total	**64**	**2024**	**1028**	**10552**

The Mandals construct is historic, and scholars think that it is built by Maharshi Vyasa. In the Mandala construct group of Richas form a Sookta (सूक्त). Collection of a few Sooktas becomes an Anuvaka (अनुवाक) or Verse, and collection of a few Anuvakas becomes one Mandala. With Mandala construct, Rigveda Samhita consists of eighty-five Anuvakas across ten Mandalas. For this reason, Rigveda is also called as Dashatayi (दशतयी). At the beginning of every Sookta, there is a mention of the Seer

(द्रष्टा ऋषि), Devata, Chhanda and Viniyoga or appropriation. The table below explains the Mandala constructs,

Mandal	Anuvaka	No. of Sūktas	No. of Richas (Mantras)
1	24	191	2006
2	4	43	429
3	5	62	617
4	5	58	589
5	6	87	727
6	6	75	765
7	6	104	841
8	10	92+11[3]	1716
9	7	114	1108
10	12	191	1754
Total	**85**	**1028**	**10552**

Any Richa in Rigveda is referenced by providing sequence number of Mandala, followed by sequence number of Sookta, followed by sequence number of Richa within that Sookta. As an example, Rg. 10.5.7 indicates the 7th Richa from the 5th Sookta in the 10th Mandala.

Including Valakhilya Sooktas, in Rigveda, there are total 1119 Sooktas.

---

[3] Additional 11 sooktas in 8th Mandala are called Valakhilya sooktas (वालखिल्य).

According to indexing done by Sage Shaunaka, there are total a total of 10,428 Richas, while with normal indexing, there are 10,552 Richas in Rigveda.

Division of Mandalas

In Mandala construct of the Rigveda, the Mandals are of two categories. Gotra also called Lineage Mandal (गोत्र मण्डल) and Mishra also called mixed Mandal (मिश्र मण्डल).

In Gotra Mandal the Seer of the entire Mandala is one Rishi or the lineage of that Rishi alone. Mandalas 2, 3, 4, 5, 6, 7, and 8 are Gotra Mandalas. The First Sookta in Gotra Mandal is Agni (Fire) Sookta and the second Sookta is Indra Sookta. Some Mandalas also include praises and greatness of the main seer of the lineage. Lineages for these Mandalas include,

Mandala	Lineage	Mandala	Lineage
2	GritSamad (गृत् समद)	3	Vishvamitra(विश्वामित्र)
4	Vamadeva, Gautama (वामदेव, गौतम)	5	Atri (अत्रि)
6	Bharadvaj (भरद्वाज)	7	Vasishta (वसिष्ठ)
8	Kanva Angiras		

	(कण्व आङ्गिरस)

In Mishra Mandala, different Seers contribute to different parts of Sooktas in that Mandala. Mandalas 1, 9 and 10 are Mishra Mandalas.

In the first Mandala, there are 16 seers. They are said to be seers of 100 Sooktas and hence called Shatarchin (शतर्चिन्).

In the ninth Mandala, there are 9 seers (or lineages of 9 seers). These are, Agastya, Angiras, Atreya, Kasyapa, Kanva, Bharadwaja, Vasishta, Vaishvamitra and Bhargava (अगस्त्य आङ्गिरस आत्रेय काश्यप काण्व भारद्वाज वासिष्ठ वैश्वामित्र भार्गव).

In the tenth Mandala, there are 152 seers. Sooktas 1 to 129 have more than 10 Richas and are called Maha Sooktas (महासूक्ते). Sooktas 130 to 191 have less than 10 Richas, and are called Kshudra Sooktas (क्षुद्रसूक्ते).

Scholars also believe that Mandalas 2 to 8 are more ancient, while Mandalas 1, 9 and 10 are relatively newer.

Women Seers in Rigveda

Contrary to modern belief, women were also extremely intelligent and had equal authority in Vedic era. Seers for many Richas are women. Women seers are called Brahmavadinis or Rishikas (ब्रह्मवादिनी or ऋषिका). Apala, Visvavara, Shasvati, Romsha, Ghosha, Lopamudra, Yami,

Godha (अपाला, विश्ववारा, शश्वती, रोमशा, घोषा, लोपामुद्रा, यमी, गोधा) are some of the Rishikas for Rigveda.

Admiration for Rigveda

While all Vedas are important and respected, Rigveda has received higher admiration amongst all the Vedas. One of the Richas in Purusha Sookta (Rg. 10.90.9) describes that from the Yajna, first the Rigveda, then the Yajurveda and then the Saamveda got created. Since Rigveda was created first, it is respected more. In Yejurvedic rituals, Mantras from the Rigveda are chanted in the beginning. All Brahmin texts refer to Richas from Rigveda to enforce their statements. Many Richas in Rigveda appear in other Vedas (with some changes in some cases).

Comprehensiveness of Rigveda

As we discussed, Rigveda or any other Vedas are not merely texts meant for rituals. This is evident from the fact that the Richas in Rigveda are revealed through people (seers) from different parts of the society. These seers include Brahmins like Vashishtha, Vamadeva, etc., Kshatriyas like Pruthu Vainya, Sudas, Yauvanashva, etc. Vaishyas like Vatsapri Bhalandan, Gandharvas like Vishvasadrisha, as well as Rakshas like Trishiras Tvashtra. We have already seen many women seers as well, who were also from different parts of the society.

It is very evident that the social status or Varna was not defined by the birth, but rather by abilities and accomplishments. People with commitment and extended study (Tapa) were able to attain status of Rishis in Vedic era.

Focus on Dharman or righteousness is more to empower the society and establish order in the order. Study of Vedic text clearly demonstrates that the knowledge is not limited to any particular race, religion or society, but rather it is available to the entire human race.

Rigveda Brahmanas

Brahmana texts provide additional explanation of the Yajna process described in Rigveda Samhita. Two of the Rigveda Brahmanas are available today. These are Aitareya Brahmana and Kaushitaki Brahmana. Aitareya Brahmana provides description of Rajasuya Yajna and Soma Yaga. It also describes the process of Coronation of emperors.

The Brahmanas were composed later than the Samhita of the Rigveda. They are considered to be the oldest texts of Hindu philosophy and provide insights into the ritualistic practices, sacrificial ceremonies, and philosophical concepts of the Vedic period. The Rigveda Brahmanas are commentaries and interpretations of the hymns in the Rigveda and contain detailed explanations of the rituals and symbolism associated with the Vedic sacrifices.

There are three main Brahmanas associated with the Rigveda: the Aitareya Brahmana, the Kaushitaki Brahmana, and the Shankhayana Brahmana. These texts are written in prose and include discussions on cosmology, ritualistic practices, social customs, and spiritual concepts.

The Rigveda Brahmanas are considered authoritative texts for understanding the rituals and religious practices of the Vedic period and are studied by scholars and practitioners of Hinduism to gain insights into the ancient Vedic traditions and their philosophical underpinnings.

The Aitareya Brahmana

The Aitareya Brahmana is a prose text that is considered to be one of the earliest and most important commentaries on the Rigveda, providing insights into the rituals and symbolic meanings of the Vedic sacrifices.

The name Aitareya comes from its author Rishi Mahidas, who was son of Itara. Being Itara's son, he was called Aitareya Mahidas and his writings are called Aitareya. The word Aitareya is also derived from itara which means progressing from here (ita means here) to the superior psychological planes (ra means movement).

The Aitareya Brahmana is divided into eight chapters, known as "khandas," and it is part of the larger Aitareya Aranyaka, which is a forest treatise associated with the Rigveda. The Aitareya Brahmana contains discussions on various aspects of Vedic rituals, cosmology, and philosophical concepts.

The text provides detailed explanations of the rituals and ceremonies associated with the Rigvedaic sacrifices, including the soma sacrifice and other rituals related to gods such as Agni, Indra, and Soma. It also includes discussions on the symbolism, and philosophical ideas related to these rituals. The Aitareya Brahmana discusses the structure of the universe, the creation of the world, and the nature of gods, humans, and the soul. It also touches upon topics such as ethics, social customs, and moral values.

The Aitareya Brahmana is considered an important source for

understanding the Vedic rituals, cosmology, and philosophical ideas of the ancient Vedic period. It is studied by scholars and practitioners of Hinduism to gain insights into the early Vedic traditions and their spiritual and philosophical significance.

The Kaushitaki Brahmana

The Kaushitaki Brahmana is another Brahmana text associated with the Rigveda.

The Kaushitaki Brahmana is also known as the Kaushitaki Brahmanopanishad, as it is considered a part of the Aranyaka portion of the Rigveda, which deals with the philosophical and mystical aspects of the Vedic teachings. It is divided into thirty chapters, known as "prapathakas,".

In addition to the rituals, the Kaushitaki Brahmana delves into philosophical ideas related to the nature of reality, creation, the soul, and the relationship between the individual self and the universal self. It discusses topics such as cosmogony, cosmology, and metaphysics, and provides insights into the early philosophical ideas that laid the foundation for later Hindu philosophical systems.

The Kaushitaki Brahmana is considered an important source for understanding the rituals, symbolism, and philosophical concepts of the Vedic period. It is studied by scholars and practitioners of Hinduism to gain insights into the deeper spiritual and philosophical aspects of the Vedic teachings and their significance in Hindu philosophy and spirituality.

Rigveda Aranyakas

The word "Aranyakas" comes from the Sanskrit words "aranya," which means "forest," and "ka," which means "belonging to" or "pertaining to." The Aranyakas are considered to be a subset of the Brahmanas, which are commentaries on the ritualistic practices and ceremonies described in the Vedas.

Aranyaka texts provide explanation of philosophy discussed in Rigveda. Aitereya and Sankhyayan (also called Kaushitaki) are two Aranyaka texts available for Rigveda.

Aitareya Aranyaka

The Aitareya Aranyaka is a commentary on the Aitareya Brahmana that expands on the ideas and concepts presented in the Aitareya Brahmana, providing further insights and explanations.

The Aitareya Aranyaka is divided into five chapters, each called an "Aranyaka." It contains a mix of prose and verse sections, and covers various topics related to rituals, sacrifices, and philosophical concepts. It includes discussions on cosmology, symbolism, meditation, and ethics associated with Vedic rituals. The Aitareya Aranyaka provides detailed instructions on various Vedic rituals and sacrifices, including the Agnihotra (fire ritual), Pravargya (ritual involving the drinking of Soma juice), and Jyotistoma (sacrifice involving the recitation of hymns). It describes the procedures, mantras (sacred chants), and symbolic meanings associated with these rituals.

It also discusses the creation of the universe, the nature of the cosmic elements, and the symbolism behind various rituals and sacrifices.

Kaushitaki Aranyaka

The Kaushitaki Aranyaka is also considered a commentary on the Kaushitaki Brahmana. The Kaushitaki Aranyaka is divided into fifteen chapters, each called a "Prapathaka." It contains a mix of prose and verse sections, covers various topics related to rituals, sacrifices, and philosophical concepts and includes discussions on cosmology, ethics, meditation, and symbolism associated with Vedic rituals. The Kaushitaki Aranyaka also provides instructions on various Vedic rituals and sacrifices, including the Ashvamedha (horse sacrifice), Agnihotra (fire ritual), and Somayajna (sacrifice involving the sacred plant soma). It describes the procedures, mantras (sacred chants), and symbolic meanings associated with these rituals.

Interpretations of Rigveda

Understanding exact meaning of Vedic texts is extremely difficult task. Texts such as Nirukta, Devatanukramani, and commentaries by various sages are helpful in interpreting these texts, however all such references are written thousands of years after Vedas. So, it is difficult to understand what the Seers had in mind. Any Mantra can reveal multiple different meanings.

There are various ways to interpret ancient texts. The most common ways include Traditional Interpretations, Western Interpretations, Spiritual Interpretations and Mysterious Interpretations.

Traditional interpretations focus on understand meanings of various words. Such interpretations focus on understanding ritualistic aspects. Associated Brahmanas and Shiksha texts are extensively used in such interpretations. Interpretations by Sayanacharya follows this method.

Western interpreters typically lack context of the text and again focus on translation rather than true interpretations. These interpretations are more recent and not that useful in understanding real meaning of the text.

Spiritual interpretations focus on spiritual aspects of the text. This method focuses on the fact that Vedas are Apaurusheya or not man-made. Various energies such as Indra, Agni, etc. are understood as Gods in these interpretations. Sages such as Madhvacharya and Dayananda Saraswati have followed this method of interpretation.

Mysterious Interpretations try to understand mysterious secret knowledge discussed in Vedic texts. These interpretations keep the context of given Mantra or Sūkta in mind and employ relevant meanings of words to find the meaning of the text. Using traditional or most common meanings of words in Mantras in deceiving and won't reveal true meaning. Various Mantras in Upanishad are based on Vedic Mantras. Upanishads are knowledge focused, so Mantras in Vedas can't merely be assumed to be ritualistic. Arvinda has used such focus. Focusing on the context while interpreting Mantras is really important.

Gods and Deities

Unlike current practices of worshipping humans or human forms, Rigvedic practices focused on worshipping natural forces and energies in the form of Gods or Deities. While there are Sūktas that offer praises to these Deities and pray for their grace, there is a possibility of invoking or activating these energies through vibrations created by chanting the Mantras.

The table below provides list of some of the Deities and natural energies of forces associated with them,

Deity	Associated Natural Force	Deity	Associated Natural Force
Agni (अग्नि)	Fire	Aditya (आदित्य) Savitru (सवितृ) Surya (सूर्य) Pooshan (पूषन्)	Sun
Ap (अप्)	Water	Indra (इंद्र)	Thunder
Ashwinikumar (अश्विनीकुमार)	Twilight before sunrise	Usha (उषा)	Early morning or Dawn
Ritu (ऋतू)	Seasong	Ribhu (ऋभु)	Wind or early morning light
Dyavaprithvi (द्यावापृथ्वी)	Sky and Earth	Parjanya (पर्जन्य)	Precipitation or Rain
Marut (मरुत्)	Thunder rain	Vayu (वायु)	Air

Additionally, Rigveda also mentions various Deities that are not necessarily associated with natural forces or energies.

In Rigveda, the Deities are categorized based on their location. These are Deities on the earth, Deities in the air and Deities in the heaven. In different commentaries, there are differences in locations of different Deities.

Philosophies in Rigveda

Rigveda discussed various philosophies such as, nature of Parameshvar, creation of the universe, relationship between soul and life, relationship between conscious and unconscious, various powers and energies in the nature, and so on.

Creation of the universe: Seers were curious about creation and origin of the universe. There are several Sūktas that discuss the creation. Indra-Vasuk dialogue in 10.27 describes how the universe was created from Sat and Asat. Purusha Sūkta (10.90) describes the creation through an explosion. Nasadiya Sūkta (10.129) takes and agnostic approach towards the creation.

Rebirth: Relationship between consciousness and supreme-consciousness or Jeevatma and Paramatma (जीवात्मा परमात्मा) is discussed in detail. Even when the Soul (or Atma) enters in the body, it is just part of it's journey. It enters and leaves the body as it continues it's journey. Concept of rebirth was understood in Rigvedic era and got further elaborated in Upanishadic era.

Polytheism or Monotheism: There are different thoughts about poly or mono theism discussed in Rigveda. Rigveda clearly mentions that the single supreme consciousness or Parameshwar (परमेश्वर) manifests in different forms. At the same time, as we discussed earlier, various natural forces and energies are also described as Deities in Rigveda. This leads to a confusion about poly or mono theism.

After Death: Rigveda mentions that after death, the soul (Atma) of the person travels to the swarloka (स्वर्लोक). There are many Mantras that are meant to help the Soul attain divine place (सद्गति).

Devotion: Many Sūktas in Rigveda are accepted to be devotional in nature. There are Sūktas that visualize a Deity in the form of friend, mother, father, spouce, etc. and offering prayers to him.

Mantravidya: Many Mantras in Rigveda are used to accomplish some specific purpose. These Mantras include,

- Devata Mantra: Praising God
- Shantipath: Remove bad luck
- Rakshghnogna: Destroy evil and demons
- Dukhaswapnanashan: Remove bad dreams
- Abhichar: Black magic

Mandalawise Topics

The Rigveda is divided into ten books, also known as mandalas. Each mandala contains hymns, prayers, and invocations dedicated to various deities and covers a wide range of topics. Some of the main topics discussed in the ten mandalas of the Rigveda include:

1. Mandala 1: Contains hymns mainly addressed to Agni (the god of fire) and Indra (the god of rain and thunder), as well as other gods. It includes invocations for protection, blessings, and prosperity.

2. Mandala 2: Focuses on the theme of cosmic order, with hymns dedicated to deities associated with natural phenomena such as the sun, moon, dawn, and night. It also includes hymns related to the creation of the universe and the origin of life.

3. Mandala 3: Discusses the importance of ritual sacrifices and praises various gods associated with the natural elements such as Agni (fire), Soma (a sacred plant used in rituals), and Varuna (the god of water).

4. Mandala 4: Addresses the relationship between humans and gods, including hymns that express praise, devotion, and gratitude to various deities. It also includes hymns that discuss philosophical concepts such as the nature of existence and the pursuit of truth.

5. Mandala 5: Contains hymns dedicated to various gods, including Agni, Indra, Varuna, and Vishnu. It also includes hymns that express the poet's personal experiences, emotions, and reflections on life.

6. Mandala 6: Discusses various gods associated with natural elements, such as Agni, Soma, and Vayu (the god of wind). It also includes hymns related to the importance of social order, ethical

conduct, and religious ceremonies.

7. Mandala 7: Addresses the theme of divine and human wisdom,
    with hymns that praise the gods as the bestowers of knowledge
    and enlightenment. It also includes hymns related to healing,
    protection, and blessings.

8. Mandala 8: Contains hymns that express praise and devotion to
    various gods, including Agni, Indra, and Surya (the sun god). It
    also includes hymns related to cosmic order, creation, and the
    natural elements.

9. Mandala 9: Discusses various gods associated with agriculture,
    fertility, and prosperity, such as Soma, Agni, and the Ashvins
    (twin gods of medicine and healing). It also includes hymns
    related to social and ethical responsibilities.

10. Mandala 10: Contains hymns dedicated to Agni and Indra, as well
    as other gods. It includes hymns related to the pursuit of truth,
    the importance of righteousness, and the glory of the gods.

Overall, the ten mandalas of the Rigveda cover a wide range of topics
including cosmology, theology, ethics, ritual practices, social order, and
individual devotion, providing insights into the religious, philosophical,
and cultural beliefs of the ancient Vedic civilization.

INTRODUCTION TO YAJURVEDA

Background

Yajurveda is primarily focused on process or Yajna and associated rituals and sacrifices. The work yajus comes from root word yaj which indicates yajan or worship or sacrifice. Yajurveda is the basis for Yajna and associated rituals. The Yajurveda is said to have emerged from the southern face of Lord Brahmā. It is also called as Adhvaryuveda or Adhavaraveda, since Adhvaryu is the main ritvik under whose direct guidance the entire sacrifice is performed. Its mantras are called yajus. The Yajurveda contains many essential teachings, including karma, the importance of rituals and sacrifices, and the belief in a supreme being or Brahman.

There are 101 branches (Shakhas) of Yajurved, 15 of which are related to Shukla Yajurveda and 86 are related to Krishna Yajurveda. Aditya Sampradaya represents Shukla Yajurveda while Brahma Sampradaya represents Krishna Yajurveda.

Shukla and Krishna Yajurveda

Maharshi Vyasa taught Yajurveda to sage Vaiśampāyana who further taught and spread the knowledge of the Yajurveda. Vaiśampāyana had a brilliant and beloved disciple named Yājñavalkya, who mastered the entirety of the Yajurveda. Later there was a conflict between the guru Vaiśampāyana and the disciple Yājñavalkya. As a result, sage Vaiśampāyana ordered sage Yājñavalkya to return all the knowledge back. There are two stories about returning the knowledge.

First story describes that Yājñavalkya vomited out all the knowledge.

There was a birds called Tittir (pheasant), who ate that vomit and started chanting Yajurveda. This seems to be an imagination of later devotees. There is no mention of Tittir being a bird in Vedic references to this context. There was a rishi with the name Tittiri who was a disciple of Vaishampayana. Tittiri is one "that which overcomes the foes (such as ignorance)."

The other story describes that sage Vaiśampāyana asked Yājñavalkya to return the knowledge by teaching it to other disciples. One of the main disciples was Sage Tittir. Yājñavalkya taught entire Yajurveda to Sage Tittir. As he taught back, his teaching had some differences that what he originally learnt. Since it was not taught in its exact original form, it was called Krishna or Black Yajurveda.

Primary reason for disagreement between sage Vaiśampāyana and sage Yājñavalkya was related to interpretations of the yajus. sage Vaiśampāyana interpreted the sacred yajus text with the outward focus only on rituals. A mantra has several interpretations, one of which is the outward rite. Sage Yājñavalkya did not agree to the interpretation only based on outer yajna process.

Since sage Yājñavalkya gave the knowledge back, he no longer had knowledge. He then left and did penance and worship to Sun God to learn the Yajurveda again in its purest form. Sun God was pleased with Yājñavalkya's worship and appeared in the form of horse (वाजिन्) and taught the entirety of the Yajurveda to Yājñavalkya. Being in its purest form, this was called Shukla or White Yajurveda. The Samhita was taught to Yājñavalkya by Sun God in the form of Horse or Vajin; hence it is also called Vajasaneya (वाजसनेय) Samhita.

The Shukla Yajurveda consists of hymns, while the Krishna Yajurveda contains the hymns as well as the prose formulas or mantras used during the Vedic rituals.

Yajurveda Samhita

The Yajurveda is divided into 4 decades or Dashakas, 40 Adhyayas (chapters), 331 Anuvakas, and 2088 Kandikas (Mantras). Yajurveda Mantras are Kandikas. with each chapter further divided into several sections or Kandas. The Shukla Yajurveda has 17 sections, while the Krishna Yajurveda has 86 sections.

There are 16 shakhas of Shukla Yajurveda that are are known, while 86 shakhas of Krishna Yajurveda are known. However, only two shakhas of the Shukla Yajurveda and four shakhas of Krishna Yajurveda are available today.

Some Anuvakas are completely Brahmana passages. There are some Anuvakas in which one part is Brahmana and another having Mantras.

Shukla Yajurveda

The Shukla Yajurveda Samhita is called the Vajasaneyi Samhita and is made up of seven books or Kandas. Two shakhas of Vajasaneyi Samhita are available today, which are Vajasaneyi Madhyandina and Vajasaneyi Kanva. The other shakhas are mentioned in other texts but are not available today.

Shakha	Adhyayas	Anuvakas	Verses (Kandikas)
Madhyandina	40	303	1975
Kanva	40	328	2086

Rituals in Vajasaneyi Samhita

In forty chapters The Vajasaneyi Samhita describes the following rituals[4],

Chapter	Ritual Name	Nature of Ritual
1-2	Darsapurnamas	Offer cow milk to fire. Separate calves from the cows.
3	Agnihotra	Offer butter and milk to fire. Welcome three chief seasons: Spring, Rains and Autumn.
4-8	Somayajna	Bathe in river. Offer milk and soma to fire. Offerings to deities of thought, speech. Prayer to Vishnu to harm no crop, guard the cattle, expel demons.
9-10	Vajapeya and Rajasuya	Cup of Victory, Inauguration of a King. Offering of butter and Sura (a drink of strength) to fire.
11-18	Agnicayana	Formulas and rituals for building altars and hearths for Agni yajna, with largest in

[4] Ref: https://www.vyasaonline.com/yajur-veda-2/

		the shape of outspread eagle or falcon.
19-21	Sautramani	Offerings of Masara (rice-barley liquor plus boiled millet) to fire. Expiate evil indulgences in soma-drinking. For dethroned king, for soldiers going to war for victory, for regulars to acquire cattle and wealth.
22-25	Ashvamedha	Only by King. A horse is released, followed by armed soldiers, wherein anyone who stops or harms the wandering horse is declared enemy of state. The horse is returned to the capital and is ceremoniously slaughtered by the soldiers. Eulogy to the departed horse. Prayers to deities.
26-29		Supplementary formulas for above sacrifices
30-31	Purushamedha	Symbolic sacrifice of Purusha (Cosmic Man). Nominal victim played the part, but released uninjured after the ceremony, according to Max Muller and others. A substitute for Ashvamedha (horse sacrifice). The ritual plays out the cosmic creation.
32-34	Sarvamedha	Stated to be more important than Purushamedha above. This ritual is a

		sacrifice for Universal Success and Prosperity. Ritual for one to be wished well, or someone leaving the home, particularly for solitude and moksha, who is offered "curd and ghee (clarified butter)".
35	Pitriyajna	Ritual funeral-related formulas for cremation. Sacrifice to the Fathers and Ancestors.
36-39	Pravargya	According to Griffith, the ritual is for long life, unimpaired faculties, health, strength, prosperity, security, tranquility and contentment. Offerings of cow milk and grains to yajna fire.
40		This chapter is not an external sacrifice ritual-related. It is Isha Upanishad, a philosophical treatise about inner Self (Atman, Soul). The verse 40.6 states, "The man who in his Self beholds all creatures and all things that be, And in all beings sees his Self, then he doubts no longer, ponders not.

While many of the rituals talk about various sacrifices, it is important to note that none of these sacrifices are related to actual slaughtering of any animal or human. Such slaughtering is not mentioned or promoted in

Vedas. Interpretations of many scholars with literal translations lead to such confusion. These are sacrifices of various aspects related to an individual such as ego, lust, attachments, vasanas and so on, or specific yogic activities or exercises.

Krishna Yajurveda

There are four available shakhas of the Krishna Yajurveda – Taittirīya saṃhitā, Maitrayani saṃhitā, Kaṭha saṃhitā, and Kapiṣṭhala saṃhitā. Vayu Purana mentions eighty-six shakhas, however majority of them are believed to be lost.

Shakha	Sub-Shakhas	Kanda	Prapathaka
Taittiriya	2	7	42
Maitrayani	6	4	54
Kāṭhaka	12	5	40
Kapiṣṭhala	5	6	48

Taittiriya Samhita: Amongst these Samhitas, Taittiriya Samhita is considered the principal. It is preached by Rishi Tittir. In Tattiriya branch Mantra and Brahmans are mixed. This Samhita is divided into 7 Kandas, 44 Prapathakas and 631 Anuvakas. This Samhita describes sacrifices and rituals related to Vajapeya, Rajasuya, etc. Taittiriya Samhita is also called "Apastamba-Samhita" after the Apastamba school, one of the chief schools in which this text was taught.

Maitrayani Sahnita: This is part of Maitrayani Shakha. Maitrayani Samhita separates Mantras and Brahmanas. This Samhita describes sacrifices and rituals related to Adhavar, Dashapurna Maasa, Chaturmasya, Punaradhan, Rajasuya, Soutramani, Ashvamedha, etc.

Kaathak Samhita: Kaathak Samhita is divided in 5 Kandas with Mantra and Brahman put together. Mantra portion is in 209 Anuvakas, Brahmana portion is in 287 Anuvakas and mixed portion is in 5 Anuvakas. This Samhita describes sacrifices and rituals related to Ithimika, Madhyamika, Orimika, Yajyanuvakya and Ashvamedhadyanuvachan.

Maitrayani and Kaathak Samhitas have similarities with Taittiriya Samhita.

Kapishthal-Katha Samhita: This Samhita is preached by Kapishthal Rishi. Only part of this Samhita is available today.

Yajurvedic Literature At-a-glance

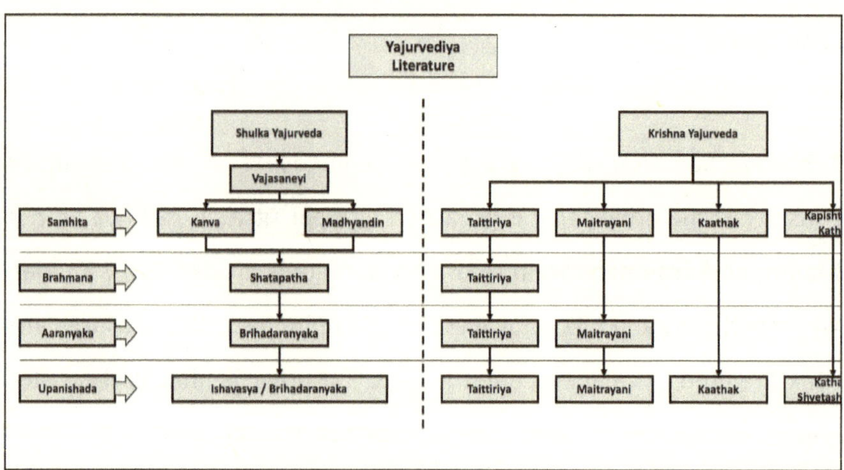

As we can see, in Krishna Yajurveda, the Mantras and the Brahmana are mixed, hence called Krishna. Whereas, in Shukla Yajurveda, Mantras and

Brahmanas are not mixed.

The main difference between the Samhitas of the Krishna and the Shukla Yajurveda is that the Vajasaneyi-Samhita contains only the Mantras for the prayers and sacrificial formulae which the priest chants. While the Samhitas of the Black Yajurveda beside the Mantras, contain a presentation of the sacrificial rites belonging to them, as well as discussions on the same.

In the Krishna Yajurveda Samhitas, that are intended for the use of the Adhvaryus, include the sacrificial rites for priests to perform as well as the prayers and the formulae. This leads to understanding that the Samhitas of the Krishna Yajurveda are older than the Vajasaneyi-Samhita. Only later the Yajurveda-theologians probably felt the necessity of having a Samhita, consisting only of Mantras analogous to the other Vedas, as well as a Brahmana separate from it.

The differences between the single Sarnhitas of the Yajurveda may have been for the priests, yet for us they are quite inessential. Black and White Yajurveda are probably not very distant from each other. A short description of the contents of the Vajasaneyi Samhita gives an idea of the contents and character of the Samhitas of the Yajurveda in general.

Some Important Topics Discussed in Yajurveda

- **Saptarshis:** Shukla Yajurveda (34.49) mentions Saptarshis and further (34.55) explains these Saptarshis as seven sages that represent specific psychological powers which are located within the body.

- **Shudras and Knowledge:** Yajurveda clearly states (26.2) that the sage should share the secret knowledge to all the persons, regardless of their status, profession or familiarity. The blissful knowledge should be taught to the shudra as well.

> *So that I may speak the blissful Word to the masses of the people,*
>
> *to the brahmana and the rajanya, to the shudra and the vaishya,*
>
> *to our own men and to the stranger. Dear may I be to the devas and to the giver of the sacred gifts here. May this my wish prosper; may that be mine.*

- **Self-Discipline:** In verse (19.30) Shukla Yajurveda provides a formula to attain the truth (or true knowledge), which begins with self-dedication or Vrata. Word Vrata is traditionally translated as austerities or rituals, however correct meaning of vrata is any vow or firm purpose. To accomplish anything of value, one must have the purpose, discipline, and dedication, which is nothing but the Vrata. Verse 19.30 says,

> *By vrata one becomes consecrated (diksha); by consecration one obtains grace (dakshina),by grace, faith andby faith, Truth is obtained.*

Concept of Yajna

Many literal translations explain Yajna as outward rituals, which may not be the most appropriate interpretation. Concept of Yajna is also inward bound or an inner act. We have already discussed that Yajna in general means a process of accomplishing something of value.

The Brahmana composer Rishis knew that it requires a person with great mental or psychological aptitude for performing the inner yajna. There are several clear mentions stating the primary importance of inner yajna.

Some references include:

- **Aitareya Brahmana (2.6.3):** "Yajamana is the sacrificial altar (yupa), he is the stone or rock, Agni is the womb of the gods; born of the offerings made through agni, the womb of gods, the yajamana with the body of gold rises upward to the world of heaven. . . . . ."

- **Taittiriya Samhita (1.6.7.4):** Both Rigveda and Yajurveda describe Indra killing the demon Vrtra with his Vajra. Taittiriya Samhita (1.6.7.4) explains this event symbolically.
  "Yajna is the thunderbolt vajra, the enemy of man is 'want, desire or thirst for objects and passions (kshud)'. In that he fasts and does not eat (i.e., he does not accede to the desires), he straightway smites with a bolt the enemy 'want'."

- **Taittiriya Samhita (1.5.2.10):** The sacrificial cake purodasha Yajamana, offering (ahuti) is the pashu."

- **Taittiriya Samhita (1.7.6):** Sacrificer is the sacrifice. Yajamana offers all he has, all he is to the gods. . . . Agni is all-gods. . . . he offers himself as the pashu of the Agni shomiya rite the gods perfect him."

- **Taittiriya Samhita (1.8.9):** Refers to the svayamkrta vedi, the altar made by oneself and svayamkrta idhma, the fire made by oneself. These phrases refer to the inner yajna, since the altar and fire in the outer yajna are made by priests.

Some important symbolisms related to Yajna and sacrifices include,

Term	Meaning	Deeper Meaning
go, gau	Cow	go represents particular type of Light or Knowledge. For this reason, word "go" is used in the context of sunlight as well.
ashva	Horse	Ashva represents the vital energy which the devas can grant.
adri	Hill	Adri is used to represent the force or beings of ignorance
apah	Water	Apah indicates the divine energies flowing from the heights, purifying all mankind
nadi	River	Nadi is the flowing current of energies.

Yajurveda Brahmanas

The term "Brahmana" is derived from the Sanskrit word "Brahman," which refers to the ultimate reality or the divine essence that underlies all of existence. The Brahmanas provide detailed explanations and instructions for performing Vedic rituals and sacrifices and contain many stories that illustrate important philosophical and religious concepts.

Yajurvediya Brahmanas include Taittiriya Brahmana of Krishna Yajurveda and Shatapatha Brahmana of Shukla Yajurveda.

Shatapatha Brahmana:

The Shatapatha Brahmana is associated with the Shukla Yajurveda and is one of the largest and most comprehensive of the Brahmanas. It contains detailed explanations and instructions for performing Vedic rituals and sacrifices, and provides insights into the social, political, and religious practices of ancient India. The Shatapatha Brahmana contains many stories including story of the sage Yajnavalkya and his dialogues with the philosopher king Janaka.

One of the most notable features of the Shatapatha Brahmana is its emphasis on the symbolism and meaning behind the Vedic rituals and sacrifices. The text interprets each ritual as representing a cosmic reality or principle and provides deep insights into the nature of the universe and the human condition.

According the Madhyandin shakha, this Brahmana is divided into fourteen books, or Kandas, 100 Adhyayas, 68 Prapathakas, 483 Brahmanas and 7624 Kandikas. This is more widely spread in northern India.

As per Kanva shakha this Brahmana has 17 Kandas, 104 Adhyayas, 435 Brahmanas and 6806 Kandikas. This is more widely spread in southern India.

Importance of Shatapatha Brahmana

Spiritual
- Yajna is most important action in life. It's way of life.
- Mind and speech are important for completing any

	yajna.
Historic	• King Janamejaya from Kuru dynasty • Aruni – the Royal teacher of Panchal • Reference to Kurukshetra as holy place for yajnas
Language	• Pros format • Bridge between Vedic Sanskrit grammar and classical Sanskrit grammar
Literature	• References of Ramayana and Mahabharata • Foundation for many Pauranik literature • Many characters from Kalidasa's literature
Scientific	• Concepts of electron and proton • Mentions of wind, earth, etc.
Cultural	• Yajna as foundation • Mention of 33 types (Koti) of devata o 8 Vasu + 11 Rudra + 12 Aditya + Indra + Prajapati
Lifestyle	• Importance of (hard) work and Tapa • Truthful behavior
Creation	• Creation of universe through Yajna performed by the Prajapati

The Flood of Manu

Shatapatha Brahmana describes a story of the flood of Manu. Biblical story of Noah's Ark and the Matsya Purana show parallels to the flood of Manu described in this Brahmana.

While Manu was taking bath one morning, a small fish requested Manu to move him to a bowl, as he was too small and the other fish would eat him. In return the fish promised to tell Manu how to save the world. After Manu moved the fish to a bowl, the fish kept on growing bigger and bigger always requesting a bigger space. He quickly grew too big requested to be placed into the River Ganga. The fish then proceeded to instruct Manu to build a ship that would hold all the animals when the great flood came. Manu did as he was told by the fish and saved the animals. The fish is thought to be a manifestation of Pajrapati.

The Secret of Fire

Many Kandas describe the fire sacrifices for Fire God, Agni. This implies an importance placed on Agni in early Vedic religion to help maintain the order of the universe. Agnicayana or Building of the Sacred Fire Altar, is described in detail in the sixth, seventh and eighth kandas. Agnicayana is one of the oldest rituals which is still performed. This twelve-day ritual is premised upon attaining vitality, offspring, or immortality. Before beginning the elaborate ritual, seventeen priests work for months to ensure the proper required preparations are completed. Particular attention is paid to the detail of the layers of the bricks to construct the fire altar (vedi). Historically, over the twelve days of ritual sacrifices are made to the god Vayu (wind) and Agni (fire), purification rites for the patron are performed, construction of the fire altar, oblations of water and ghee.

Many sets of Mantras conclude by saying: "Thus this comes to make up the whole Agni and the whole Agni comes to be the space-filler; certainly whosoever knows this, thus comes to be that whole Agni who is the space-filler."

Taittiriya Brahmana:

This is the Brahmana associated with the Taittiriya shakha. It contains mantras that are recited during Vedic rituals and sacrifices, as well as explanations and instructions for performing various rituals and ceremonies. The Taittiriya Brahmana also contains many stories that illustrate important philosophical and religious concepts, such as the nature of the soul and the ultimate reality of the universe.

The Taittiriya Brahmana is composed by Rishi Tittiri who was disciple of Save Vaishampayana. It has 3 Kandas. First Kanda has 78 Anuvakas, Second Kanda has 96 Anuvakas and third Kanda has 179 Anuvakas.

Importance of Taittiriya Brahmana

Spiritual	• Discussion about many Yajnas such as Agnyadhan, PurushaMedha, Vajapeya, Somayaga, Rajasooya, etc.
Legends	• Stories of Nachiketa, Pralhad, Agastya, etc. • Stories related to Deities, Nature and Yajna • Many details about constellations (Nakshatras)
Historic	• King Janaka • Aaruni • Kingdoms of Kuru and Panchal
Lifestyle	• Moral and ethical values • Food habits

- Truthful speech

Yajurveda Aranyakas

Aranyakas are generally the concluding portions of the several Brahmanas, but on account of their distinct character, contents and language deserve to be reckoned as a distinct category of literature. Some Aranyakas are partly included in the Brahmanas themselves, but some are recognized as independent works. Aranyaka literature is rather small as compared to the Brahmanas. Whereas the Brahmanas deal with the huge bulk of sacrificial paraphernalia which represents Karma-Kanda, the Aranyakas and Upanishads, on the other hand, chiefly deal with the philosophical and theosophical speculations which represent Jnana-Kanda.

The word Aranyaka comes from word Aranya which indicates forest. Aranyaka can be loosely translated as Forest Texts[5]. It is defined as araṇye bhāvamiti āraṇyakam (अरण्ये भावमिति आरण्यकम्). While Brahmanas describe yajnas done at home or in the city, Aranyakas discuss rituals performed away from the society and in the forest. Aranyakas are more focused on detachment, meditation, contemplation, etc. Detachment from fruits of actions by following rules the of Brahmacharya is important in Aranyaka. Penance, meditation, self-study (self-analysis),

---

[5] अरण्येतदधीयीतेत्येवों वाक्यों प्रवक्ष्यते - तैसिरीय आरण्यक
अरण्य अध्ययनाच्च ऐतद् आरण्यकमइसत - सम्बन्ध वार्तिक

contemplation, yajna, etc. are activities related to Aranyaka.

Aranyakas are vanaprasthāśrama texts that focus on knowledge (jnan kanda). Aranyakas explore symbolic meaning and mystery of Brahmanas with philosophical focus. For this reason, Aranyakas are also called Rahasya Brahmanas. Aranyakas lead to topics and teachings of Upanishadas. For good understanding of mature knowledge in Upanishadas, analysis of knowledge provided in Aranyakas is essential. Hidden secrets behind Yajnas and other rituals are understood in Aranyalas through detached study. Some of the ancient Upanishads are found as part of Aranyaka texts.

Brihadaranyaka

Brahadaranyaka from Shukla Yajurveda forms six chapters of Shatapatha Brahmana. It discusses Atmatatva in details. Concepts like Brahman, Atma, and Punarjanma (rebirth) are explained in Brahadaranyaka. Many topics are revealed through the Saje Yajnavalkya's discussion with others such as Maitreyi, Gargi, Janak, Shakalya and others.

Maitrayani Aranyaka

Maitrayani Aranyaka is associated with Krishna Yajurveda Maitrayani Samhita. It consists of 7 Prapathakas and 73 Khandas. Self-realization is an important topic along with detailed discussion about OM. Om itself is Pranava and the Brahman. The Brahman can be worshipped through worship of Om alone. Various vital energies that are identified as varies deities are nothing but Brahman. Maitrayani Aranyaka discsusses deities such as Brahma, Vishnu, Rudra, Prajapati, Agni, Varuna, Vayu, Indra and

Chnadra[6], which means everything in the universe is nothing but Brahman. This concept is further elaborated in various Upanishadas.

Taittiriya Aranyaka

The Taittiriya Aranyaka is associated with Taittiriya shakha of Krishna Yajurveda. It is divided into ten chapters or Prapathakas, also known as Aranas and 170 Anuvakas. It deals with style of fire-brick pilling, Mahayajnas, recitation of the Vedas (including sacred thread, daily prayer, sacrifice to the ancestors and the Brahmayajna), procedures for performing several other homas and Yajnas, mantras used in the Pravargya rituals, records of the Pitrimedha Yajna, and the Upanishadic thoughts of the Taittiriya and Mahanarayana Upanishad.

Out of the ten chapters the seventh, eighth and ninth chapters form Taittiriya Upanishad and tenth chapter forms Mahanarayana Upanishad. Taittiriya Aranyaka discusses the eternal truths and highest level of philosophical thoughts are mentioned in a symbolic manner.

Other important topics include,

- Shramana, the word used for Buddhist monks, is explained in this Aranyaka as Ascetic person.
- The process of Pancha-Maha-Yajna (Yajna for Deva/deities, Pitru/ancestors, Bhoota/all beings, Manushya/humans and

---

6 त्वं ब्रह्मा त्वं च वै विष्णुस्त्व ँ रुद्रस्त्वं प्रजापतिः
त्वमग्निर्वरुणो वायुस्त्वमिन्द्रस्त्वं निशाकरः

Brahman) is explained.

- Concepts about continuous flow of time time and time measurement in the form of Sanvatsar, Muhurta, Din, Ratri, Paksha, Maas, etc.

- Four forms of water viz. cloud, thunder, storm and rain

- Six types of water viz. rain water, well water, pond water, river water, spring water and stored water (in pots, etc.)

Commentaries

Primary commentaries include,

- **Shatapatha Brahmana:** itarasvāmī, uvaṭa, sāyar, miīdhara, kapavandrācāyā, nīlakaṇṭha, ānantācāyā

- **Taittiriya Brahman:** sāyar, bhaṭṭabhāskara miśra

INTRODUCTION TO SAAMVEDA

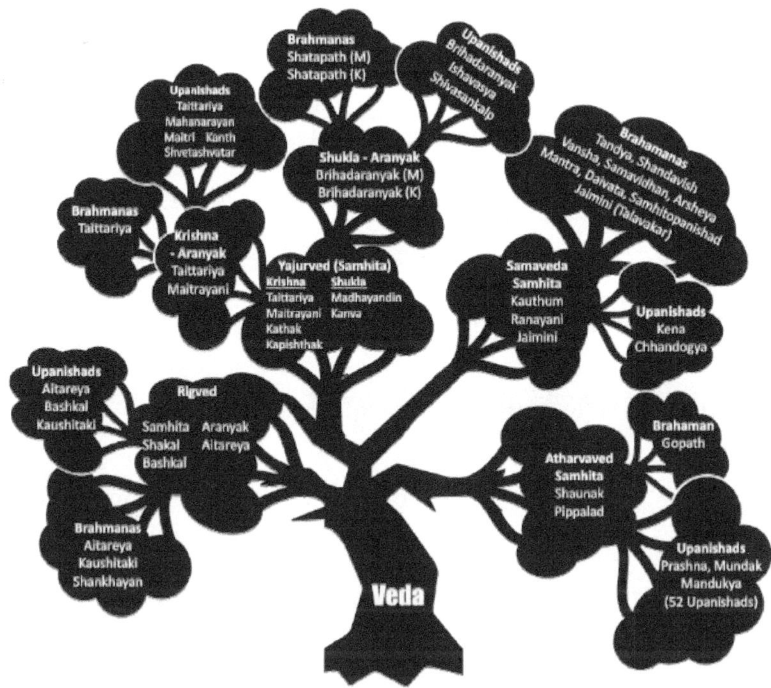

Background

The Samaveda is considered the third Veda, following the Rigveda and the Yajurveda. The word "Samaveda" means "knowledge of melodies" or "knowledge of chants."

Samaveda, as the name indicates, is Veda or Samas. Sāmnāṃ vedaḥ sāmavedaḥ (साम्नां वेदः सामवेदः). Sam indicates Richas that are sung. In Brihadaranyakapanishad, Sama has been derived by giving the meaning of 'Sa' as Rick and 'Am' as song.

सा (ऋचा) + अम (गान्धारादि स्वर) = साम

In Samaveda, the complete form of Geetika is found through the main seven swaras. Samaveda Mantras is called Sama. Samaveda Mantra portion is also called Samhita. Samaveda Samhita is found in written format.

While a Sama is in the Richa singing format, the Richa has more importance. Same Richa is sung in different ways. At various rituals, these Richas are sung in specific manner. This leads to an understanding that the art of singing (and music) is evolved from Samaveda.

The Samaveda consists of a collection of hymns and melodies that were originally chanted during rituals and ceremonies. It is primarily a collection of verses from the Rigveda, set to musical melodies and arranged in a poetic form. These verses are known as Samans or Samagana.

The Samaveda is closely associated with the ancient Indian musical tradition, as it provides the musical notations and patterns for chanting the verses. The melodies and rhythms of the Samaveda were believed to have a profound spiritual and transformative effect when performed correctly.

The preservation and transmission of the Samaveda has been traditionally carried out through an oral tradition, with the verses and melodies passed down from generation to generation by Vedic priests called Samavedis. Today, the Samaveda continues to be an important text in Hindu religious rituals and ceremonies, and its melodies and chants are still practiced and performed in traditional Vedic chanting.

Maharishi Vyasji preached Vedas to his four disciples named Pail, Vaishampayan, Jaimini and Sumantu. The tradition of Samaveda begins with Jaimini. Jaimini taught it to his son Sumantu, Sumantu taught it to his son Sunvan and Sunvan taught his son Sukarma. In this way the study tradition of Samveda is going on. In Vedatrayi consisting of prose, verse and song, the song portion or Geetibhag is called Samaveda.

Samaveda Branches

There is a mention of having thousand branches of Samaveda in Mahabhashya. "Sahastravartma Samvedah". On the occasion of Samatarpan, the Tarpan is offered to the thirteen Samavediya Acharyas as follows,

1. Ranayana	2. Satyamugri-Vyasa	3. Bhaguri-Aulundi
4. Goulmulavi	5. Bhanuman	6. Aupamanyava

7. Daral	8. Gargya	9. Savarni
10. Varshagani	11. Kumuthi	12. Shalihotra
13. Jaimini		

Out of these, today only three branches preached by Ranayan, Kuthumi and Jaimini, are available, known as Ranayaniya, Kauthumi and Jaimini respectively. The Ranayaniya branch is popular in South, Kauthumiya in Vindhyachal to North India. In Kerala, the study and teaching of the Jaimini branch is dominant. Most of India follows the Kauthumiya branch. Due to its pronunciation difference, two methods are seen viz. Nagarpaddhati and Madrapaddhati. The Govardhani system by Ranayan is seen in Kashi.

Some difference can be seen in the songs of Kauthumiya and Ranayaniya branches. Although the tradition of running the work of both the branches from the Kauthumiya branch has started due to the fact that the hymns of the Ranayaniya branch have not been published from anywhere till date, however, the claim of having separately written songs is of the Ranayaniya branch.

Importance of Samaveda

Various texts have described the Samaveda to be an important text in Vedic literature. Some of the references include,

- sāmāni yo vetti sa veda tatvam (सामानि यो वेत्ति स वेद तत्वम्) meaning, one who knows Samaveda, knows secrets of Vedas – Brihad-devata.

- vedānām sāmavedosmi (वेदानाम् सामवेदोस्मि) meaning, I am Samaveda within all the Vedas – Bhagvad Geeta
- yo jāgāra tamu sāmāni yanti (यो जागार तमु सामानि यन्ति) meaning, only the one who is awake (awakened) can understand Samaveda - Rigveda

Samaveda Mantra portion consists of archika and songs. Archika is also divided into Purarchika and Uttararchika. Altogether 1875 mantras are recited in 27 chapters in both. Out of which, except 75 mantras, all the rest are found in the Shakal Samhita of Rigveda. Scholors believe that the 75 mantras are part of lost branches like Shankhayan etc.

Purvarchika is divided in 6 chapters called Prapathakas. These 6 chapters are grouped in 4 groups based on the topics discussed. These groups are,

- Aagneya   1st Prapathaka   Ruchas related to Agni
- Aindra   2nd to 4th Prapathakas   Ruchas related to Indra
- Pavamana   5th Prapathaka   Ruchas related to Soma
- Aranyaka   6th Prapathaka

Further, 1st through 5th Prapathakas form Gramagaan, meaning Samas sung in public (or in the village/city). The 6th Prapathaka forms Aranyagaan, meaning Samas sung in forest or away from crowded place. The Aranyaka consists of 5 sections known as Arka, Dwandva, Vrata, Shukriya and Mahanamni.

Uttararchika consists of 9 Prapathakas and 1225 Richas or Mantras. Based on the topics discussed, these Prapathakas are grouped in 7 groups. These groups are Dasharatra, Sanvatsara, Ekaha, Ahina, Satra, Prayashchitta, and Kshudra.

Samaveda Brahmanas

Sayana bhashya mentions 8 Brahmanas of Samaveda. These are,

- Praudh or Tandya Brahmana
- Shadvinshabrahmana
- Samavidhanabrahmana
- Arsheyabrahmana
- Devatadhyaybrahmana
- Chhandogyaupanishad-brahmana
- Samhitopanishad-brahmana
- Vamshabrahmana

Additionally, there are references to many more Brahmanas from Jaiminiya branch. However, these texts are not available.

Tandya Brahmana is the largest Brahmana and has 25 chapters. Being the largest Brahmana, it is also called as Mahabrahmana and for having 25 chapters, it is also called Panchavinsha (twenty-five) Brahmana.

Shadvinshabrahmana has 6 cahpters. This Brahmana is said to be 26th chapter of Tandya Brahmana, hence the name Shadvinsha (meaning 26) Brahmana. Mantras to remediate various undesirable or evil events are described in this Brahmana. Words such as Shoolapanaye, Chakrapanaye, Dandapanaye, etc. describing gods in human form are found in this Brahamana. These might be the foundations for various forms of gods we see today.

Samavidhanabrahmana consists of 3 chapters. The first chapter describes sequence of the creation. It symbolically describes that Brahma imagined Samas as food for its seven kids who were satisfied by seven swaras of Sama. From seven Swaras, Krushta, Prathama, Dvitiya, Tritiya, Chaturtha, Mandra and Atiswaar, species Deva, Manava, Pashu, Gandharvas, Apsaras, Pitruganas/birds, Asuras were satisfied respectively.

Arsheyabrahmana is divided in 6 chapters. It describes various Rishies associated with names of Sama. Naming Samas based on names of Seers gives it name Arsheya. Arsheya means relating or belonging to or derived from a Seer. It also means "of sacred descent".

Chhandogyaupanishad-brahmana consists of 10 chapters. First two chapters describes rituals such as wedding and remaining 8 chapters form the Upanishada.

Samhitopanishad-brahmana has 5 parts and explains secrets of Sama Samhita.

Vamshabrahmana has 3 parts to it and describes traditions of studying Samaveda.

Samaveda Aranyakas

Texts built and practiced in forests (Aranya) are called Aranyaka. Aranyakas move the comprehension of Veda from ritual aspects (Karmakanda) to knowledge aspects (Jnankanda). Aranyakas appear after

Brahmanas and before Upanishadas. In few cases Upanishadas are part of Aranyaka itself, making it difficult to distinguish between Aranyaka and Upanishada texts. Samaveda has two Aranyaka texts, Talavakar or Jaiminiyopanishad Aranyaka and Chhandogyaranyak.

Talavakara Aranyaka consists of three chapters (Prapathakas) and is considered an important bridge between the ritualistic Brahmanas and the philosophical Upanishads. It contains discussions on various topics such as rituals, symbolism, meditation, and cosmology. The Talavakara Aranyaka is often studied in conjunction with the associated Brahmana and Kena Upanishad. The Kena Upanishad is also considered a part of the Talavakara Aranyaka.

Together these texts discuss philosophical concepts such as the nature of the self (Atman) and the ultimate reality (Brahman).

Chhandogya Aranyaka comprises ten chapters (Prapathakas) and is traditionally attributed to the sage Uddalaka Aruni. It is closely connected to the Chhandogya Upanishad, one of the principal Upanishads and an integral part of the Aranyaka.

The Chhandogya Aranyaka deals with various philosophical and spiritual topics, including rituals, sacrifices, meditation practices, cosmology, and the nature of reality. It contains profound teachings on the nature of the self (Atman) and its relationship to the ultimate reality (Brahman).

INTRODUCTION TO ATHARVAVEDA

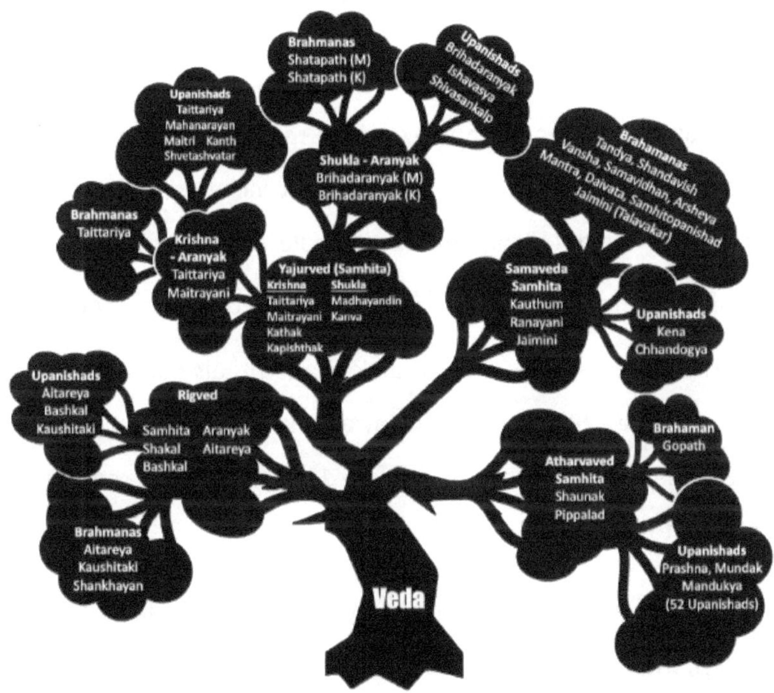

Background

Atharvaveda, the fourth Veda, is much different from the first three. Initially it was not accepted as a Veda due to various reasons, however later, due to same reasons it was accepted as fourth Veda, as we will see. Atharva Deva has many distinct and unique characteristics. It provides practical or applied knowledge that most people can relate to and apply in their day-to-day life activities. Mantras and rituals related to prayers, curing diseases, weddings, family, society, self-defense and so on, are discussed in Atharvaveda.

Topics that are related to most common man all the way to supreme kings are discussed in Atharvaveda. Since it includes topics related to common man and not highly educated people, sarcastically this Veda was also called grāmayājin (ग्राममयाजिन्). This Veda got categorized as a folk literature and it describes many practices and rituals that are commonly in use even today. (Black) magic, mantra, tantra, threads, puppets and so on, are some of the techniques discussed in Atharvaveda that we see in the society today.

While Atharvaveda was initially not accepted as a Veda to be part of Vedatrayi, the Gopatha Brahmana, which is widely accepted as summary of all Vedas, proclaims Atharvaveda to be the most important Veda. Padmapurana also states that even when days, stars, constellations, etc. are not in favorable position, one can accomplish desired results merely chanting Atharvaveda Mantras. Other Pauranik literature also mentions importance of Atharvaveda in similar words.

Abhicharvidya (अभिचारविद्या) is predominantly introduced and discussed in Atharvaveda. Practical aspects of these techniques to protect self from others using these techniques as well as using these techniques to defeat or harm enemies is acceptable approach discussed here. We also find specific saṃkalpa (संकल्प) or resolution for destroying an enemy. Since Atharvaveda is focused on addressing topics for common people, many prevailing black magic, trntra vidya and other techniques are mentioned as rituals. While rituals in Rigveda are sātvika in nature, many (so to say) inferior tāmasika rituals are found in Atharvaveda.

In addition to deities from Rigveda, many new deities based on magical formulae are found in Atharvaveda. Additionally, many of the holy deities from other Vedas are used as instruments to fulfill certain desires.

For performing any four Ritvijas, one representing each Veda, are required. The Ritvija representing Atharvaveda is called Brahma and is said to be the chief Ritvijs. He is expected to have knowledge of all other Vedas and thorough understanding of entire Yajna ritual.

- Brahma Veda named after it's Ritvij, Brahma,
- Atharvaangirasa Veda named after two Rishi dynasty, Atharva and Angira. Atharva provides all peace mantras and Angira provides ceremonial mantras.

  Atharva also indicates noble people while Aangiras indicates teacher (acharya) that teaches violent activities and rituals. The name Atharvaangiras indicates combination of good and violent mantras.

- Bhrigvangiras Veda as it was spread by Bhrigu Rishi who was disciple of Angira Rishi

- Kshatra \ Raj Veda as it describes various rituals related to coronation of the king

- Bhaishajya Veda as it provides details about medical science

- Yatu Veda as it describes various magical powers

- Chhandoveda

- Maheeveda

- Etc.

After getting acceptance as fourth Veda, Brahmanas for Atharvaveda were developed.

Branches of Atharvaveda

Just like other Vedas, multiple branches of Atharvaveda are found. According to Katyayana's Sarvanikramani, there are 15 branches of Atharvaveda, while Patanjali only mentions 9 branches. These 9 branches are widely accepted by scholars. These branches are, 1. Paippalad (or Pippalad), 2. Taud, 3. Maud, 4. Shaunakiya, 5. Jajala, 6. Jalad, 7. Brahmavada, 8. Devadarshi and 9. Charanavaidya.

Of all these branches, texts for only Paippalad and Shaunikiya are available today, of which for Paippalad branch only the Samhita is available.

Types of Samhitas

Various Samhitas of Atharvaveda are available. Based on how these are taught and the application of its Mantras, Samhitas are categorized based as,

- **Arshi Samhitas:** These Samhitas are collection of Mantras that are acquired by Rishis through oral and "Guru-Shishya" tradition. These are also known as Rishi Samhitas. Shaunakiya Samhita which is available today is of this category.

- **Acharya Samhita:** Samhitas that are taught by Rishis to their disciples after Upanayan (threading or initiation) samskara are Acharya Samhitas.

- **Vidhi Prayog Samhitas:** When specific Mantras are used for a specific purpose or ritual, those Mantras may be repeated or mixed with other Mantras. Such collection of Mantras is Vidhi Prayog Samhita.

It can be concluded that Arshi Samhitas are core (root) Samhitas. Acharya Samhitas are condensed forms for Acharya Samhitas and Vidhi Prayog Samhitas are applications of those Samhitas.

Atharvaveda of Rishis

Rishi for most of the Suktas in Atharvaveda is Rishi Atharva. Atharva means unshaken, steady, stable, undisturbed, or focused. Other Rishis mentioned connect to Rishi Atharva. We can see names such as Atharvachrya, Atharvangira, etc. Names of many Rishis seem to be indicators of qualities than individuals.

Atharvaveda of Samhitas

Various texts mention 9 different Samhitas of Atharvadeda. However, 7 of these 9 Samhitas are not available today. Pippalad and Shunak are 2 Samhitas that are available.

Paippalad Samhita:

This Samhita is mentioned in text called Prapanchahridaya. According to this text, this Samhita is from Rishi Pippalad. Only one handwritten copy of this Samhita was found in Kashmir region, and was written in the Sharada script. Scholars think that Paippalad Samhita is more ancient than Shaunakiya Samhita. This Samhita is divided in 20 Kandas, 923 Kandikas and 3837n Mantras.

Paippalad branch does not have its own Brahmana texts. Upanishadas like Prashna, Mundaka are associated with this branch. This branch is spread mostly in Orrisa region through oral tradition.

Shaunak Samhita

Shaunaka Samhita is from Rishi Shaunak. It consists of 20 Kandas, however scholars believe this to be of 18 Kandas. 19th and 20th Kandas are Khila (or appendix) Kandas. These 20 Kandas consist of 736 Sūktas and about 6000 Mantras.

- Kanda 1 to 7 have smaller Sūktas consisting of 1 to 8 Mantras
- Kanda 8 to 18 have larger Sūktas consisting of 21 to 89 Mantras
- Kanda 19 and 20 and Khila Kanda

Following key subjects are discussed in these Kandas,

- 14th Kanda is Vivaha Kanda
- 15th Kanda is Vratya Kanda
- 16th and 17th are Abhichara Kanda
- 18th Kanda is Pitru or Antyeshti Kanda

Other Texts Associated with Atharvaveda

There are various texts associated with this Veda. These include, Brahamana, Upanishada, Shiksha, Kalpa, etc.

Atharvaveda Brahmanas

There are two Brahmanas associated with Atharvaveda. These are Gopatha Brahmana and Paippalada Brahmana.

Gopatha Brahmana:

The Gopatha Brahmana is considered an important text for understanding the rituals, symbolism, and practices of the Atharvaveda. It provides insights into the religious and cultural traditions prevalent during the Vedic period.

The Gopatha Brahmana consists of two sections: the Purva Khanda (first part) and the Uttara Khanda (second part).

The Purva Khanda focuses on rituals and sacrificial ceremonies associated with the Atharvaveda, including hymns, chants, and their interpretations. It provides details and explanations regarding the rituals performed during that time.

The Uttara Khanda of the Gopatha Brahmana deals with various topics such as the origin of the universe, cosmology, medical practices, and magical rituals. It contains discussions on the nature of reality, the power of mantras, and the role of deities in different aspects of life.

Atharvaveda Upanishadas

Atharvaveda has largest number of Upanishadas. Known and accepted Upanishadas associated with Atharvaveda include,

- Prashna
- Mundaka
- Mandukya
- Atharvashirsha
- Atharvashikha
- Brihadjabal
- Nrusinhatapini
- Narada-Parivrajak
- Seeta
- Sharabh
- Mahanarayana
- Ramarahasya
- Ramatapini
- Shandilya
- Paramahamsa Parivrajak
- Annapurna
- Surya
- Atman
- Pashupat
- Parabrahma
- Tripuratapini
- Daivi

- Bhavana

- Braahma

- Jabal

- Ganapati

- Mahavakya

- Gopal Tapani

- Krishna

- Hayagreeva

- Dattatreya

- Garuda

Let's understand topics discussed in some the Upanishadas.

Prashnopanishad: This Upanishad is associated with Paippalad shakha. Seven sages come to Sage Paippalada seeking his guidance on Brahmagyan or supreme knowledge. These sages include Sukesha Bharadvaj, Shaibya Satyakam, Souryayani Gargya, Kausalya Ashvalayan, Bhargav Vaidharbhi, and Kabandhi Katyayan. Sage Paippalad asks them to serve in his ashram for one year to test their sincerity and desire to learn. Once proven, Sage Paippalad answers 6 questions for those sages. This discussion forms Prashnopanishad. Through this discussion, Sage Paippalad provides philosophical insights on topics such as the process of the creation of the universe, founding principles (or devatas) of human life, immortality, form of meditation, importance of meditation, concept of Omkara, Concept of liberation, and so on.

Mundakopanishad: Taught through Guru-Shishya Parampara starting from Brahma to Atharva to Angirasa to Bharadvaj to Satyavaha to

Shaunak, this Upanishad destroys ignorance (avidya) and provides Brahmagyan that leads one to liberation. Famous statement, Satyameva Jayate which means "only thuth becomes victorious", is from Mundakopanishad. Details about Para and Apara Vidya are discussed in this Upanishad.

Mandukyopanishad: This is the smallest Upanishad consisting of only 12 Mantras; however, this is considered to be the most sacred with lot of deep sacred knowledge. Ayatma Brahma, which is one of the Mahavakyas, is from this Upanishad. This Upanishad discusses many important philosophies through explanation of 4 aspects of divine sound Om. Om consists of 4 sounds, A, U and M, followed by silence. These are related to 4 stages of awareness, Jagriti or awake stage, Swapna, or dream, Sushupti or deep sleep and Turiya which is deep meditative stage. Four stages of Atman corresponding to these stages are described as Vaishvanara, Taijasa, Prajnya and Parabrahama respectively.

Topics Discussed in Atharvaveda

Focus of Atharvaveda is less on Yajna rituals and more on topics associated with day-to-day life matters for common people. There are several topics which are categorized as Yatu or Abhichara, which means magic or employment of spells for a malevolent purpose. Additionally, there are several other topics discussed in Atharvaveda.

- **Abhicharani:** Abhicharani topics deal with magic or employment of spells for a malevolent purpose. Topics such as violence-oriented acts such as Shatrunashan or destruction of the enemy, Sadrishya or creating objects with clay or wood and performing magic on them, directed towards someone, destroying ghosts, etc. are included in Abhicharani sūktas.
- **Pushtiprad:** These are topics related to strengthening a person.

These include Paushtik, Ayushya, Rajakarma, etc. Solutions such as chanting various Mantras for personal benefits and improving mental health/strength, removing effect of poison, etc. are also discussed.

- **Bhaishajyani:** These are medical treatments describing various diseases, cure and prevention for those, hereditary problems, medicinal properties of various trees and herbs, etc. are discussed under Bhaishajyani. Various viruses, bacteria, microorganisms, and others causing health issues are mentioned as Rakshasas or demons. Based on the descriptions of these "demons", modern day scientists have been able to relate these to such viruses, etc.

- **Ayushyani:** Ayushani topics discuss various solutions for living long and healthy life. Dirghayusūkta, Apamrityuvaransūkta, etc. are Sūktas discussing these topics.

- **Paushtikani:** These are sūktas that discuss how to live healthy and acquire various strengths.

- **Rajakarmani:** These are sūktas that describe various procedures for kings, army, etc. Procedures and rituals related to coronation, expanding kingdom, acquiring new kingdoms, praises for kings, enemy destruction, praises for weapons, etc. are some of the topics under Rajakarmani.

- **Strikarmani:** These sūktas describe various aspects related to women. Topics such as marriage, pregnancy, spells to influence other men or women, taking away beauty or potency of other women, blessings for good kids and family, protection of fetus, removing defects in the fetus, healthy delivery and many other women related topics are addressed in Strikarmani sūktas.

- **Prayashchittani:** Prayashchittani describe various sūktas related to punishments for various sins, mistakes, inappropriate actions, etc.

- **Sammanasyani:** These sūktas address aspects for building and maintaining healthy relationships with family, friends, society, teachers/students, etc. Some of the sūktas include topics such as social unity, compromises with enemies, controlling anger, winning with majority, etc.

There are various other topics including spiritual, charitable, praises of Brahmins, Yajna related sūktas, death rituals, and many more.

Deities in Atharvaveda

While Atharvaveda has many deities described in Rigveda (such as Agni, Indra, Vayu, Surya, etc.), many new deities related to Abhichara are found in Atharvaveda. These deities are said to be inferior to deities described in Rigveda. Classes of these new deities include Diseases, Vampires, Constellations, Gandharvas, Krityas, Ghosts, Snakes, (रोग पिशाच नक्षत्र गन्धर्व कृत्या भूते सर्प), etc. Using mantra, tantra, magics, etc. these deities are employed for removal of pains and problems.

Medical Science

Atharvaveda has various suktas that are used as remedy for certain diseases. These suktas are called Bheshaj or Upachar Suktas. Various herbs, rituals, mantras, etc. that are used for remediation or cure, are generally called Bheshaj.

Ayurveda, which is foundation of ancient Indian medical practices, is sourced from Atharvaveda and hence it is accepted as Upveda of Atharveveda. Since Atharvaveda is more ancient that Ayurveda, Ayurveda has more details about medical practices. Advance medical science developed by Charak and Sushrut is based on these texts.

UPAVEDAS

The Upavedas are a set of knowledge systems that supplement and further elaborate on the fundamental teachings of the four Vedas. Upvedas provide insights into specific domains of knowledge. There are traditionally four Upavedas associated with the respective Vedas:

1. **Ayurveda (associated with Rigveda):** Ayurveda focuses on the knowledge of health and medicine. It encompasses a holistic approach to well-being, combining physical, mental, and spiritual aspects. Ayurveda includes principles of diet, herbal medicine, surgery, and various therapeutic practices to promote a balanced and healthy life.

2. **Dhanurveda (associated with Yajurveda):** Dhanurveda provides the knowledge of military science and archery. It includes teachings on warfare, strategy, martial arts, and the use of weapons. While not as extensively documented as other Upavedas, Dhanurveda reflects the historical context where societies valued warfare skills and strategic acumen.

3. **Gandharvaveda (associated with Samaveda):** Gandharvaveda, deals with the knowledge of music, dance, and performing arts. It explores the aesthetic dimensions of sound, rhythm, and melody, emphasizing the spiritual and transformative aspects of artistic expression. It also provides guidelines for the performing some rituals those involve music and dance.

4. **Sthapatyaveda (associated with Atharvaveda):** Sthapatyaveda also called Shilpa Veda, is an ancient Indian system of architecture and construction that forms a part of the broader field of Vastu Shastra. The name Sthapatyaveda comes from the term "Sthapati," meaning "architect" or "builder," and the term "Veda," which refers to knowledge or science. Sthapatyaveda addresses the science of architecture and building, which is deeply rooted in the philosophical and cultural fabric of India. It encompasses not only the technical aspects of building but also

integrates principles of harmony, aesthetics, sustainability, and spiritual well-being. This holistic approach to architecture is aimed at creating spaces that are in harmony with the natural world, the cosmos, and the energies that pervade our environment.

While these Upavedas are associated with specific Vedas, their boundaries can overlap, and interpretations may vary. Additionally, the Upavedas enrich Vedic knowledge by providing a comprehensive framework that addresses various aspects of human life, from health and warfare to arts and governance. The teachings of the Upavedas continue to influence and inspire diverse fields of study, contributing to the holistic understanding of life and the universe in the Vedic tradition.

The Ayurveda

Ayurveda, often referred to as the "Science of Life," is an ancient system of holistic healing that originated in the Indian subcontinent. The word "Ayurveda" is derived from the Sanskrit words "Ayur" meaning life. This comprehensive system not only addresses the treatment of diseases but also provides guidelines for maintaining optimal health and balance in all aspects of life.

The roots of Ayurveda are deeply embedded in the ancient Indian scriptures, particularly the Vedas, with the Rigveda containing some of the earliest references to healing practices. Ayurveda evolved over centuries, influenced by the philosophical and spiritual traditions. Its principles were systematically organized into Samhita texts by rishis such as Charaka and Sushruta. These Samhitas are used even today in Ayurvedic medicine practices.

Unlike western medical treatments that focus curing a disease (or a medical condition) by analyzing symptoms, Arurveda takes more holistic approach. The Ayurveda is founded on the concept of the "Panchamahabhutas" or the five elements – earth, water, fire, air, and ether. These elements combine to form three "Doshas"

- Vata (associated with air and ether)
- Pitta (linked to fire and water)
- Kapha (related to water and earth)

Maintaining a balance among these doshas is crucial for overall health, and imbalances are believed to be the root cause of diseases.

Prakriti – The Individual Constitution: One of Ayurveda's key concepts is the understanding of individual constitution, or "Prakriti." Each person is believed to be born with a unique combination of the doshas, influencing their physical, mental, and emotional characteristics. Recognizing one's Prakriti is vital for designing personalized wellness practices, including diet, lifestyle, and therapeutic interventions.

Diagnostic Techniques: Ayurvedic diagnosis involves a holistic assessment, considering not only physical symptoms but also mental and emotional aspects. Practitioners use techniques such as pulse reading (Nadi Pariksha), tongue examination, and observation of bodily constitution to identify imbalances and determine appropriate interventions.

Treatments: Ayurvedic treatments focus on restoring balance to the doshas through a combination of natural remedies, lifestyle adjustments, dietary changes, and therapeutic practices. Herbs, minerals, and dietary guidelines are often prescribed based on an individual's constitution and the nature of the imbalance.

Prevention Focus: The emphasis is not only on curing diseases but also on preventing them while living a healthy and long life. Ayurveds prescribes various daily practices called "Dinacharya" as well as occasional or seasonal practices called Ritucharya, to maintain overall well-being and maintain an overall balance.

Ayurveda also deals with ***yoga and meditation practices***. The three disciplines work synergistically to enhance physical, mental, and spiritual health. Yoga postures (asanas), breathing exercises (pranayama), and meditation are integral components of Ayurvedic wellness.

Ayurveda principles are relevant in modern lifestyle. The holistic approach, emphasis on personalized care, and integration of natural remedies align with the growing interest in alternative and integrative medicine globally.

Dhanurveda

Dhanurveda is an ancient Indian martial art and science of warfare that finds its roots in Vedic literature. The term "Dhanurveda" is derived from the Sanskrit "Dhanu" meaning bow or weapon. Dhanurveda encompasses various aspects of archery, weaponry, military strategy, and the ethical principles guiding the use of force.

Dhanurveda is mentioned in several ancient texts, including the Vedas, Puranas, and epics like the Mahabharata. The Rigveda, one of the oldest Vedic scriptures, contains hymns praising the prowess of archers and warriors. The Yajurveda and Atharvaveda also make references to the science of weaponry and military strategy.

Dhanurveda is a physical discipline, which is also deeply rooted in philosophical and ethical principles. The use of force is considered a last resort, and warriors are expected to adhere to dharma (righteousness) on the battlefield. The Arthashastra, an ancient treatise on statecraft attributed to Chanakya, incorporates Dhanurveda principles and provides guidelines for rulers on military strategy, espionage, and governance.

Training in Dhanurveda involves the mastery of various weapons, including bows, arrows, swords, spears, and maces. Archery, in particular, holds a prominent place, and the skill of accurately shooting arrows is considered a hallmark of a proficient warrior. Techniques for hand-to-hand combat, the use of shields, and battlefield maneuvers are also integral parts of Dhanurvedic training.

Dhanurveda played a crucial role in ancient Indian warfare, especially during the times of the Mahabharata and the Ramayana. The epic heroes like Arjuna and Rama were skilled archers, and the narratives often highlight the strategic use of weapons and martial arts in battle.

Dhanurveda gives detailed categorization of various weapons based on how those are used as well as impact it can create. There are various mass impact weapons called as Astras, described in Dhanurveda that resemble today's bombs and missiles.

Inspite of offering knolwdge of warfare, Dhanurveda carries symbolic and spiritual significance. The bow, a central weapon in Dhanurveda, is often considered a metaphor for the disciplined mind, and the arrows represent focused intent. The Bhagavad Gita, a sacred text within the Mahabharata, uses the metaphor of the bow and arrow to convey profound spiritual teachings.

With the advent of gunpowder and modern weaponry, traditional martial arts like Dhanurveda experienced a decline. However, in recent times, there has been a revival of interest in these ancient disciplines. Efforts are being made to preserve and transmit the knowledge of Dhanurveda through specialized training programs, workshops, and research initiatives.

Dhanurveda is not merely a set of combat techniques; it is deeply woven into the cultural fabric of India. Traditional dance forms like Kathak often incorporate elements of Dhanurveda in their movements, showcasing the fluidity and precision associated with the martial art. Festivals and events that celebrate the rich cultural heritage of India often feature demonstrations of Dhanurvedic skills.

Gandharvaveda

Gandharvaveda describes Vedic knowledge related to music, performing arts, and aesthetics. Gandharvaveda is often associated with the Gandharvas, celestial musicians, and is considered a part of the broader Vedic tradition. While there might not be a specific text known as "Gandharvaveda," the term is used to encompass the musical and artistic knowledge found in Vedic literature.

The Sama Veda, contain hymns and verses dedicated to music and the divine aspects of sound. These references lay the foundation for

Gandharvaveda as the Vedic knowledge associated with the arts. The Atharvaveda also contains verses related to musical incantations.

Gandharvas: Gandharvas, the celestial beings associated with music and arts are often depicted as singers and musicians in the court of gods. The Gandharvas are considered experts in the art of music, and their influence is believed to inspire and enhance the aesthetic experience.

Bharata Muni's Natyashastra, an ancient Indian text on performing arts, is often considered an extension of Gandharvaveda. Natyashastra provides detailed guidance on music, dance, drama, and aesthetics, offering a comprehensive understanding of the performing arts within the Vedic tradition.

Gandharvaveda explores the concept of Rasa, which refers to the emotional essence conveyed through artistic expressions. Rasa theory, foundational to Natyashastra, categorizes the emotional impact of different artistic elements, contributing to the overall aesthetic experience.

The Sama Veda, known for its musical verses, provides a glimpse into the musical traditions of ancient India. The musical elements in the Vedas include chanting of mantras with specific tones and melodies, reflecting the sacred and ritualistic use of music in Vedic ceremonies.

Spiritual Practice: In the Vedic tradition, music and the performing arts are not merely forms of entertainment but are considered spiritual practices. The recitation of Vedic mantras with specific musical intonations is believed to have a profound impact on the mind, leading to spiritual elevation.

Indian Classical Music: The principles and aesthetics outlined in Gandharvaveda have influenced the development of classical music in India. The ragas, talas, and melodic structures found in classical music traditions can be traced back to the foundational concepts embedded in Gandharvaveda.

The study of Gandharvaveda is not just about mastering artistic techniques but also involves exploring the philosophical dimensions of sound, rhythm, and expression. It delves into the relationship between the individual, the cosmos, and the divine, using the arts as a medium for spiritual exploration.

Sthapatyaveda

Sthapatyaveda describes science of architecture and construction that forms a part of the broader field of Vastu Shastra. The word Sthapatyaveda comes from Sanskrit word "Sthapati" which means "architect" or "master builder". Thus, Sthapatyaveda is the science of architecture and building, deeply rooted in philosophy and cultural of India. It encompasses not only the technical aspects of building but also integrates principles of harmony, aesthetics, sustainability, and spiritual well-being. This holistic approach to architecture is aimed at creating spaces that are in harmony with the natural world, the cosmos, and the energies that pervade our environment.

The origins of Sthapatyaveda can be traced back to texts, including the Rigveda. However, it is in the later Vedic texts and post-Vedic literature, such as the Vishwakarma Vastushastra, Mayamatam, and Manasara, that the principles of Sthapatyaveda are more explicitly articulated. These texts provide detailed guidelines on the art of building, covering temples, palaces, and residential buildings, as well as the planning of cities and villages.

At the core of Sthapatyaveda is the concept of Vastu Purusha Mandala, a metaphysical plan that integrates the five elements of nature (earth, water, air, fire, and space), directions, and astrology, with human existence. The Vastu Purusha Mandala is a symbolic representation of the cosmos, with each part corresponding to a specific aspect of the physical and spiritual world. Buildings and spaces designed according to this mandala are believed to enhance the well-being of their inhabitants by aligning with cosmic principles.

Design Principles and Applications: Sthapatyaveda emphasizes several key principles in design, including:

- **Orientation:** The direction of a building is crucial, with east-facing entrances being particularly auspicious due to the significance of the rising sun in Indian culture.
- **Proportion and Scale:** The texts specify measurements and proportions to ensure aesthetic harmony and balance in the design.
- **Energy Flow:** The layout of spaces is designed to ensure a smooth flow of energy, or prana, within the building.
- **Material Selection:** Natural materials are preferred, and their use are guided by considerations of sustainability, local availability, and the health of the occupants.

The modern society is showing increasing interest in Sthapatyaveda and Vastushastra, particularly among those seeking sustainable and spiritually meaningful approaches to architecture. Its principles are being adapted and applied in the design of residential, commercial, and public buildings, often blending traditional wisdom with contemporary architectural practices. Despite of this interest the applications of Sthapatyaveda continues to face challenges. Critics argue that strict adherence to ancient texts may not always be practical or relevant in the rapidly changing modern landscapes. Moreover, the interpretation of Vastu principles can vary, leading to different approaches to design that may not align with the original intent of Sthapatyaveda.

VEDANGAS

The Vedangas are the "limbs" or auxiliary texts of the Vedas. These are a group of six additional subjects that evolved to support the study and understanding of the Vedic texts. These disciplines play a crucial role in elucidating and preserving the correct pronunciation, interpretation, and application of Vedic knowledge. The Vedangas are considered essential for the proper comprehension and practice of the Vedic rituals and philosophies. The Vedangas include,

1. **Shiksha (Phonetics):** Shiksha deals with the phonetic aspects of the Vedas. It provides rules for proper pronunciation, accentuation, and intonation during the recitation of Vedic hymns. Shiksha aims to preserve the oral tradition of the Vedas by guiding the correct articulation of sounds and ensuring the transmission of Vedic knowledge without distortion.

2. **Chandas (Metrics):** Chandas is concerned with the meters and rhythms. It explores the various poetic meters used in Vedic compositions, emphasizing the importance of maintaining the correct meter during recitation. Understanding Chandas is crucial for preserving the poetic structure and musicality inherent in Vedic verses.

3. **Vyakarana (Grammar):** Vyakarana is the study of grammar and linguistic aspects. It focuses on the rules governing the formation and interpretation of sentences in the Vedic texts. A thorough knowledge of Vyakarana is essential for accurate comprehension and interpretation of the Vedas, ensuring the preservation of their intended meanings.

4. **Nirukta (Etymology):** Nirukta is concerned with the etymology and interpretation of Vedic words. It provides explanations for the meanings of archaic or obscure terms found in the Vedic texts, helping to elucidate the symbolic and ritualistic significance of words used in Vedic rituals and hymns.

5. **Kalpa (Rituals):** Kalpa deals with the procedures and rituals

outlined in the Vedas. It provides guidelines for conducting various ceremonies, sacrifices, and rituals in accordance with Vedic traditions. Kalpa includes three sub-divisions:

    a.   Shrauta Sutras describe rituals for public ceremonies

    b.   Grihya Sutras describe domestic or at-home rituals

    c.   Dharma Sutras describe ethical and legal principles

6. **Jyotisha (Astronomy and Astrology):** Jyotisha focuses on the study of astronomy and astrology in the context of Vedic rituals and calendars. It provides insights into celestial movements, auspicious timings for rituals, and the calculation of solar and lunar calendars. Jyotisha ensures the alignment of Vedic practices with astronomical phenomena.

Personification of various phenomena and other aspects is very common aspect of ancient traditions. With this practice, the Vedas are personified as the Vedic *Purusha* or a human form. The Vedangas are considered as the limbs of the Veda *Purusha*. Just like a human cannot be properly understood without studying its limbs, Vedas cannot be properly understood without studying Vedangas. Personification in human form provides a framework is in the subtle realm of knowledge.

Each of the Vedanga corresponds to (or represents) a particular body part of the Veda *Purusha*. This mapping includes,

1. The Shiksha is considered to be the 'Nose'. The nose is associated with inhalation and exhalation which is critical aspects of sound or speaking Shiksha being the science of sound, is considered to be the nose of the Veda Purusha.

2. Kalpa is considered to be the hands. The hands are instrument of action and Kalpa deals with various ritualistic actions.

3. Vyakarana is considered to be the face. The face creates impression as well as forms the base of receiving and transmitting knowledge. Vyakarana is the prescribes various rules and guidelines of the of Sanskrit, leading the creating the impression and communicating the knowledge. Hence the Vyakarana is the face.

4. Nirukta forms the ears. Nirukta deals with the meaning and origins of the words that the ears listen to, Nirukta is the ears of the Veda Purusha.
5. Chhanda forms the legs. Chhanda defines the meters which defines the length (or distance) of various verses (Mantras), Chanddas is said to be the legs of the Veda Purusha.

We will now dive deeper and understand more details about the Vedangas.

Shiksha

Shiksha, as one of the Vedangas, is the discipline that deals with phonetics and the correct pronunciation of the Vedic texts. It is considered essential for preserving the oral tradition of the Vedas and ensuring the accurate transmission of Vedic knowledge from one generation to another. Shiksha provides a set of rules and guidelines for the proper articulation of sounds, intonation, and pronunciation during the recitation of Vedic hymns.

The primary purpose of Shiksha is to maintain the purity of Vedic recitation. It ensures that the exact phonetic nuances and intonations specified in the Vedas are preserved, preventing any distortion or misinterpretation. The significance of Shiksha lies in its role as a foundational discipline for the correct chanting of Vedic mantras, which are believed to have a profound impact on both the individual and the cosmos.

Important aspects of Shiksha include,

1. Phonetic Elements: Shiksha provides instructions about correct pronunciation of the phonetic elements. This includes the accurate articulation of vowels, consonants, sibilants, and other phonetic components. Each Vedic sound has a specific place of origin in the mouth, a particular manner of articulation, and a defined level of force or intensity, all of which are meticulously outlined in Shiksha.

2. Accentuation (Svara): Shiksha is particularly concerned with the correct application of accentuation or "svara,". Accentuations play a crucial role in conveying the intended meaning of the Vedic verses and ensuring the proper rhythm and musicality of the recitation.

3. Intonation and Melody: Shiksha also addresses the melodic aspects of Vedic chanting. It guides the proper modulation of pitch and tone. The meters or "chandas," are closely linked to Shiksha.

Shiksha is not just a theoretical study; it is meant to be applied in practical recitation. Students of the Vedas undergo training in Shiksha to master the correct pronunciation and intonation. This training often involves direct oral instruction from a qualified teacher, emphasizing the importance of the guru-shishya (teacher-student) tradition in Vedic education.

Accurate pronunciation is critical in Vedic rituals, where the power of the spoken word is believed to have a direct impact on the efficacy of the ceremony. Shiksha ensures that the mantras recited during rituals maintain their sanctity and potency, upholding the spiritual significance of the Vedic practices.

Shiksha plays a vital role in the preservation of the Vedic tradition. By maintaining the correct pronunciation and intonation, Shiksha contributes to the continuity of the oral transmission of Vedic knowledge, safeguarding the authenticity of the ancient texts.

Chandas

Chandas refers to the study of meters and prosody in Vedic literature. It deals with the rhythmic and metrical aspects of Vedic hymns and chants. The study of Chandas is crucial for understanding the structure and rhythm of Vedic verses. The meters used in Vedic poetry contribute to the musicality, memorability, and oral transmission of the texts.

Chandas classifies Vedic meters into various types, each with its specific structure and rules. The most common meters are Gayatri, Trishtubh, Anushtubh, and Jagati, among others. Each meter has a defined number of syllables, called matras, in each verse.

Chandas helps in analyzing the syllabic structure of Vedic verses, which is fundamental for maintaining the integrity of the text during oral recitation. The study of Chandas involves understanding the arrangement of short and long syllables within a meter.

Chandas contributes to the musical and melodic quality of Vedic chants. The rhythmic patterns, when recited with the correct intonation, enhance the aesthetic and spiritual experience of the Vedic verses.

Chandas is intimately connected to Vedic rituals and ceremonies. The specific meters chosen for recitation in rituals are believed to have spiritual significance, and the correct application of Chandas is vital for maintaining the sanctity of these practices.

The theoretical aspects of Chandas are compiled in texts known as "Chandas Shastra." These texts provide rules, classifications, and examples of different meters, serving as a guide for students and scholars studying Vedic prosody.

Vyakarana

Vyakarana refers to the study of grammar and linguistic structure. It is one of the six Vedangas that support the study and understanding of the Vedas.

Vyakarana is derived from the Sanskrit root "vyakri," which means to analyze or explain. Vyakarana serves the purpose of systematically analyzing and explaining the rules of grammar and linguistic structure found in the Vedas. Its primary goal is to ensure the correct interpretation, pronunciation, and usage of Vedic texts.

While thre are several Sanskrit grammarian, Panini, an ancient Sanskrit grammarian, is renowned for his comprehensive work on Sanskrit grammar called the "Ashtadhyayi." This important text, composed around the 4th century BCE, is considered the foundation of Vyakarana. It systematically organizes the rules of Sanskrit grammar in a concise and logical manner.

Vyakarana covers various aspects of Sanskrit grammar, including phonetics (Shiksha), morphology (prakriya), syntax (vakya), and semantics (artha). It provides rules for the formation of words, sentences, and the proper use of grammatical elements.

Important aspects of Vyakarana include,

1. Sandhi: Sandhi refers to the rules for combining two or more words. Vyakarana provides guidelines on how words interact when they come together, including rules for vowel and consonant changes in word junctions.
2. Karaka: Karaka system provides a linguistic framework that assigns specific roles or functions to different elements within a sentence. This system helps in understanding the relationships between words and their grammatical functions in a sentence.
3. Nirukta: While Nirukta is a separate Vedanga focused on etymology, Vyakarana also includes aspects of word analysis and interpretation. Vyakarana helps in understanding the meanings of words and their contextual usage.
4. Accentuation: Vyakarana provides rules for Vedic accentuation, which involves the correct placement of stress or pitch in Vedic chanting. Understanding the rules of accentuation is crucial for preserving the proper pronunciation and meaning of Vedic verses.

The study of Vyakarana extends beyond Vedic literature and has contributed significantly to the development of linguistic sciences in India. Panini's Ashtadhyayi is not only a grammar manual for Sanskrit but also a foundational work that influenced subsequent grammarians and linguists worldwide. Vyakarana plays a crucial role in Vedic rituals, where the precise pronunciation of mantras is considered essential. The knowledge of grammar ensures that the correct phonetic elements are maintained during Vedic recitation, contributing to the effectiveness of the rituals.

Like other Vedangas, Vyakarana contributes to the preservation of the Vedic tradition. By providing rules for grammatical accuracy, it ensures that the Vedas are transmitted with precision, maintaining their linguistic integrity over generations.

Nirukta

Nirukta, one of the Vedangas, is the discipline focused on etymology, the study of the origin, formation, and meaning of words in the context of the Vedas. It is an essential branch of Vedic studies, serving to provide insights into the meanings of Vedic terms, especially those that may be archaic or have symbolic significance. Most Sanskrit words are derived from the root verb called Dhatu. Many words have different meanings depending on the context. In such situations, knowing the origin of the word and relating it to given context becomes crucial.

Nirukta is derived from the Sanskrit root "ni" (down) and "rukti" (speech or expression), suggesting an examination or interpretation of words. The primary purpose of Nirukta is to explain the meanings of Vedic words and expressions found in the Vedic texts, facilitating a deeper understanding of the ritualistic and philosophical aspects of the Vedas.

The foundational text of Nirukta is attributed to the ancient sage Yaska, who authored the "Nirukta," an influential commentary on Vedic words and their meanings. Yaska's Nirukta systematically examines words, their derivations, and their contextual significance within the Vedic corpus. Nirukta involves the analysis of words, their roots, prefixes, and suffixes. It explores the etymological aspects of Vedic terms, helping to unravel the historical and linguistic layers embedded in the language of the Vedas.

Nirukta also seeks to understand the symbolic meanings, allegorical references, and cultural connotations associated with specific words to help interpret right meaning. As the Vedas were transmitted orally for centuries, maintaining the correct meanings of words was crucial. Nirukta contributes to the preservation of the intended meanings of Vedic verses, preventing misinterpretations and ensuring the continuity of the Vedic tradition.

The Vedas contain archaic and symbolic language that may be challenging to interpret without a proper understanding of the cultural and linguistic context. Nirukta helps unravel these archaisms and provides insights into the symbolic language used in Vedic rituals and hymns. Nirukta is particularly important in the analysis of Vedic mantras. It helps identify the root meanings of individual words within a mantra, shedding light on the precise intentions and nuances embedded in the verses.

Beyond linguistic analysis, Nirukta can offer spiritual and philosophical insights by revealing the subtle meanings and metaphysical concepts embedded in Vedic terminology. It aids in understanding the philosophical underpinnings of Vedic thought.

Kalpa

Kalpa refers to the study of rituals, ceremonies, and ethical conduct as prescribed in the Vedas. Kalpa is derived from the Sanskrit root "kri," meaning "to do" or "to perform." Kalpa focuses on the procedures, rituals, ceremonies, and ethical practices outlined in the Vedas. Its primary purpose is to provide guidelines for the correct performance of Vedic rituals, ensuring that they adhere to traditional principles and ethical standards.

Kalpa is traditionally classified into three main branches:

1. Shrauta Sutras: Deal with rituals performed in public ceremonies, especially those involving the Soma sacrifice.
2. Grihya Sutras: Concerned with domestic rituals, including rites of passage, family ceremonies, and daily practices.
3. Dharma Sutras: Cover ethical and legal principles, guiding individuals on righteous conduct and social duties.

Shrauta Sutras: Shrauta Sutras provide detailed instructions for the performance of elaborate and grand rituals, especially the Soma sacrifice. These rituals were typically conducted in public with the participation of priests and attendees. Shrauta Sutras offer guidelines on the construction of altars, chanting of mantras, and specific actions to be performed during these rituals.

Grihya Sutras: Grihya Sutras focus on domestic rituals performed within the household. These include rites of passage such as birth ceremonies, marriage rituals, and funeral rites. Grihya Sutras offer guidelines for householders to observe daily and occasional rituals, ensuring the harmony and well-being of family life.

Dharma Sutras: Dharma Sutras are concerned with ethical and legal principles, providing guidelines for righteous conduct and social responsibilities. They address matters such as morality, justice, and duties in various aspects of life. Dharma Sutras serve as a moral code, guiding individuals in their personal, familial, and societal roles.

Kalpa plays a crucial role in Vedic rituals, where the correct performance of ceremonies is believed to have cosmic significance. The rituals are seen as a means of maintaining cosmic order (rta) and fostering a connection between the human and divine realms. Kalpa provides detailed instructions on the materials required for rituals, the specific actions to be performed, the pronunciation of mantras, and the role of different priests in the ceremonies. It emphasizes precision and adherence to tradition to ensure the efficacy of the rituals.

Kalpa also plays a crucial role in preserving the oral tradition of Vedic rituals. The guidelines and procedures outlined in Kalpa ensure the continuity of rituals across generations, maintaining the sanctity and authenticity of the Vedic tradition.

While Kalpa Vedanga primarily deals with ritualistic aspects, it also has philosophical significance. The rituals are often accompanied by symbolic meanings and allegorical interpretations that convey deeper spiritual insights and cosmic principles.

Jyotisha

Jyotisha is the study of astronomy, astrology, and related sciences. The word Jyotisha is derived from the Sanskrit root "jyot," meaning light or heavenly body. Jyotisha involves the study of celestial phenomena, including astronomy and astrology. Its primary purpose is to provide a systematic understanding of the movements of celestial bodies, the measurement of time, and the correlation between cosmic events and terrestrial life.

Jyotisha is traditionally divided into three main branches:

1. **Ganita (Mathematics):** Deals with mathematical calculations related to astronomy. Jyotisha incorporates a comprehensive study of astronomy, including the positions and movements of celestial bodies such as the sun, moon, planets, and stars. Mathematical calculations, celestial coordinates, and planetary positions are critical components of Jyotisha. It also provides methods for measuring time based on celestial movements. The day and night are divided into specific units, and the lunar and solar calendars are used for determining auspicious timings for rituals and events.

2. **Samhita (Mundane Astrology):** Focuses on predicting natural events and global affairs based on celestial observations. Samhita astrology focuses on predicting natural events and their impact on the world. It includes the study of omens, eclipses, earthquakes, and other celestial phenomena believed to influence the course of global affairs.

3. Hora (Individual Horoscopy): Concerned with personal astrology, including the preparation and interpretation of individual horoscopes. Hora astrology involves the preparation and interpretation of individual horoscopes (Janma Kundali). It considers the positions of planets at the time of an individual's birth to provide insights into their personality, life events, and

potential challenges.

Other important aspects of Jyotisha include,

- **Muhurta (Electional Astrology):** Muhurta is the branch of electional astrology. Muhurta helps in determining auspicious timings for various activities such as weddings, business ventures, and other important events based on the positions of celestial bodies.
- **Yogas:** Jyotisha incorporates the analysis of planetary combinations known as "Yogas" and potential afflictions called "Doshas." These factors play a role in determining an individual's strengths, weaknesses, and potential life outcomes.
- **Nakshatras:** Jyotisha divides the zodiac into 27 lunar mansions or Nakshatras. Each Nakshatra has specific attributes and is used in astrology for various predictive purposes, including horoscope analysis and Muhurta determination.

Jyotisha plays a crucial role in Vedic rituals, where the timing of ceremonies is often determined based on celestial observations. The positioning of celestial bodies is believed to influence the effectiveness and auspiciousness of rituals.

CONCLUSION

It is essential to encapsulate the profound depth, historical significance, and living impact of this ancient tradition. The Vedic system, with its intricate layering of texts, philosophies, rituals, and practices, offers not just a window into the spiritual and intellectual endeavors of ancient India but also presents a timeless guide to understanding the universe, life, and the self.

Through the exploration of the Vedas, Upanishads, Brahmanas, Aranyakas, Upavedas and Vedangas, this book has endeavored to unravel the complex fabric of Vedic thought, highlighting its emphasis on cosmic order (Rta), the interconnectedness of all beings, and the pursuit of truth (Satya) and righteousness (Dharma). The Vedic knowledge system is not merely an academic or religious relic; it is a living tradition that continues to influence millions of lives around the world, offering insights into ethics, mindfulness, and the pursuit of knowledge.

Moreover, the Vedic system's integrative approach to knowledge, which encompasses not only spiritual and philosophical realms but also practical domains such as mathematics, medicine (Ayurveda), and astrology (Jyotisha), underscores the holistic vision of life it proposes. This unity of knowledge reminds us of the interconnectedness of all fields of inquiry and the importance of balance between the material and spiritual, the individual and the cosmos.

As we close this exploration, it becomes clear that the Vedic knowledge system, with its profound insights and timeless wisdom, holds relevant lessons for contemporary society. In a world grappling with rapid change, environmental crises, and the search for meaning, the Vedic perspective offers paths toward harmony, sustainability, and inner peace. It encourages us to see beyond the transient, to value wisdom over mere information, and to cultivate a deeper, more holistic understanding of our place in the universe.

This book, therefore, is not just a study of ancient texts and rituals but an invitation to engage with a living tradition that offers guidance on how to live a life of purpose, balance, and harmony. As we move forward, let us carry with us the light of Vedic wisdom, illuminating our path to a more enlightened, compassionate, and connected world.

In this conclusion, we honor the ancient sages who, in deep meditative states, glimpsed the eternal truths. As we close this chapter, let us remember that the Vedas are not mere texts—they are gateways to the infinite, beckoning us to unravel the mysteries of existence, one sacred syllable at a time.

REFERENCES

- Rigveda Sanhita Hindi by Pt. Shri Ram Sharma Acharya

- Rigveda Bhashya By Maharshi Dayananda Saraswati

- Rigveda Samhita Damodar Satavalekar

- Marathi Translation of Rigveda by Dr. Siddheshwar Shastri Chitrao

- Rig Veda Sanhita By H H Wilson

- Sakshi Trust - https://vedah.com/

- World History Encyclopedia - www.worldhistory.org/TheVedas/

The author acknowledges that much of the content in this book is derived from knowledge accumulated over years of study and learning from various authorities. Given the extensive nature of these sources, specific references may not be individually cited.

Other Publications

We always hear that the Vedic scriptures are full of knowledge, but there is little effort made to understand and share the knowledge in this literature.

This book decodes various Mantras in Purusha Sukta with scientific mindset. Since this Sukta is focused on creation of the universe, the book focuses on understanding scientific aspects related to creation of the universe in the Sukta

Upcoming Publications

Bhagvad Geeta is best manual for living an inspired life. However, many people treat it as a religious text and only worship it. Few who read it, typically read it without understanding the meaning and even fewer understand the meaning but don't know how to apply it in day-to-day life.

This book uncovers various life lessons from Bhagvad Geeta that we can easily understand and apply in our day-to-day life. This book guides us with practical applications of the text.

Various human qualities and tendencies are explained along with guidance on how to control those to enrich our lives.

Find out more at
https://www.intexp.net/books

www.ingramcontent.com/pod-product-compliance
Lightning Source LLC
Chambersburg PA
CBHW022021150726
47990CB00002B/755